reversible
COLOR CROCHET
*a **new** technique*

Laurinda Reddig

INTERWEAVE.
interweave.com

Editor: Katrina Loving

Technical Editor and Illustrator: Charles Voth

Associate Art Director: Julia Boyles

Cover Design: Courtney Kyle

Interior Design: Brenda Gallagher

Photographer: Joe Hancock

Stylist: Emily Smoot

Production: Katherine Jackson

Interweave
A division of F+W Media, Inc.
4868 Innovation Drive
Fort Collins, CO 80525
interweave.com

Manufactured in China
by RR Donnelley Shenzhen.

Library of Congress
Cataloging-in-Publication Data

Reddig, Laurinda.
Reversible color crochet : a new technique /
Laurinda Reddig.
pages cm
Includes index.
ISBN 978-1-62033-338-9 (pbk.)
ISBN 978-1-62033-473-7 (PDF)
1. Crocheting--Patterns. 2. Afghans
(Coverlets) 3. Color in textile crafts. 4. Square
in art. I. Title.
TT825.R3865 2014
746.43'4-dc23
2013039901

10 9 8 7 6 5 4 3 2 1

Acknowledgments

I would not be writing this book were it not for the influence of my early crochet "teachers." I'd like to thank them all, from the Camp Fire leader who first taught me to make granny squares to all the women who shared new skills with me over the years. I also need to thank my mom, Linda, who took me to my first yarn store and taught me to sew, and my dad, Kit, who exposed me to knitting and intarsia. I'd also like to mention my grandma Diana, who passed on her love of all crafts from the time I was very young.

Thanks to my friends Katherine, Caren, Brandy, Heather, Mercedes, and others who understand that "playdate" really means "your children entertain mine while I crochet afghans!" Special thanks to my end-weaver, Carissa, my primary tester, Barbina, and my last-minute finisher, Judith. Also, thanks to the Clark County Fiber Friends for letting me bounce ideas off them, especially Julia Hosack for her crochet hooks and quilt knowledge.

Thanks to Doris Chan and Andee Graves, who coordinated the CGOA's annual design competition, which got me to send my first designs out into the world. I count those ladies among the many mentors who have generously helped me along the way, as well as Bonnie Pierce, Vashti Braha, Marty Miller, Dora Ohrenstein, and many more awesome designers who have shared their experiences and answered my (sometimes random) questions.

Thanks to the awesome team at Interweave, especially Marcy Smith, my tech editor Charles Voth, Allison Korleski (who walked me through my first book proposal), and my awesome editor, Katrina Loving.

Finally, thanks to my family for their patience, as I ignored everything else to finish this book. To my mother-in-law, Rachel, for helping with child care and listening to my rambling. To my husband, Mike, for always supporting me and not complaining (too much) about doing all the laundry and dishes during my busiest weeks. And of course, to my children, who are my inspiration and who only complained occasionally about the ever-present hook and yarn in my hands.

Dedication

For my son Griffin, who was the inspiration for my first design in this technique and whose creativity inspires me every day.

Original drawings by Griffin Reddig may be seen on page 102.

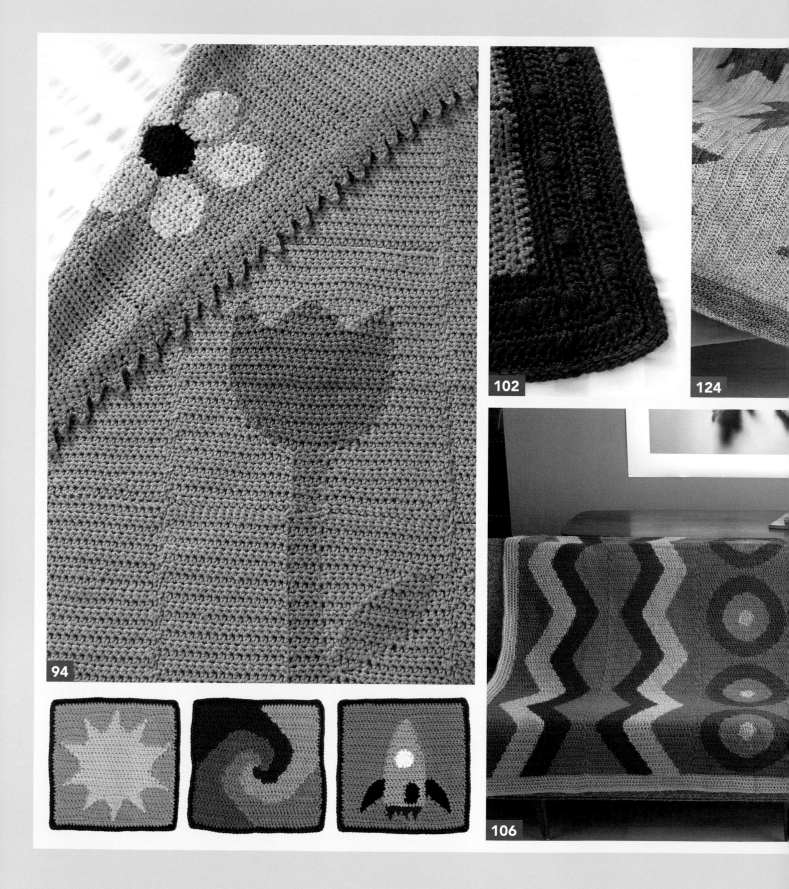

94

102

124

106

Table of Contents

Introduction

In a craft that has been around as long as crochet, we seldom come across anything truly new. Though reversible crochet colorwork may not be a brand-new idea, the technique that I have developed is the result of many years of experimentation and adapting techniques learned from others. The result is truly reversible colorwork that is not stiff and produces clean lines, which allows for a wide variety of exciting designs.

I was first introduced to crochet colorwork through tapestry crochet. A friend from high school taught me to use multiple colors and carry the yarn under stitches. I began using the technique in my crochet, but I never liked the look of the carried yarns peeking through taller stitches (such as double crochet). Many years later, when I was expecting my first baby, my father decided to knit an afghan covered in tiny intarsia animals for his first grandchild. This opened my eyes to the possibility of having a separate ball of yarn for each section of color, rather than carrying the unused colors.

When my son was a little older, I decided to make him an afghan featuring a cartoon image that was created by using intarsia in crochet. Whenever I changed colors, I simply did what made sense to me and carried the old color up inside the stitches. Unlike knitting, the thicker stitches created by crocheted fabric make it easy to hide the strands of the unused color, making them reversible.

After my son's afghan won awards at the Crochet Guild of America (CGOA) Design Competition in 2011, other crocheters began asking for the pattern. As I consulted all of the books and experts I could find, I realized that my technique was indeed different than anything else available. I began to work on writing patterns and refining the details of the reversible intarsia approach. My Reversible Rowan Tree Vest, designed in memory of my first daughter, gave me the opportunity to hone the technique and won the grand prize at the CGOA Design Competition in 2012.

When I was just beginning to get my designs published, I took an online pattern-writing class to improve my skills. The instructor suggested that I submit designs and articles to various magazines to teach the technique. But no one project could explain the entire technique, so I developed a sampler afghan with squares that would gradually demonstrate all the necessary skills. That sampler idea eventually morphed into this book, and that same instructor became my technical editor.

With this book, you can learn to create beautiful, reversible colorwork by making just a few small changes in how you work the yarn before and after color changes. So get out your hooks and start playing with color!

~Laurinda Reddig

CHAPTER 1

Getting Started

If you are reading this book, you probably already have some crochet experience, and you may be looking for a new challenge or, perhaps, a different approach to colorwork. Although the reversible intarsia technique presented in this book is not difficult (using half double or double crochet stitches), there are elements of the technique that will most likely be new to you. So, don't be tempted to skip over this first chapter, as it contains many tips and tricks, as well as the foundation information you will need to achieve fantastic reversible intarsia results.

How to Use This Book

This book is organized in a linear fashion, with twenty-eight squares that lead into ten afghan projects (each square is utilized in one or more of the afghans). The first twelve squares are the "learning" squares. They feature simple geometric designs and include extra information within the pattern text that will remind you when and how to make color changes.

Working through these first twelve squares is the best way to familiarize yourself with the technique. They slowly ease you into working with more and more colors and give your fingers a chance to learn the stitches unique to reversible intarsia. I have also included several tips and tricks to help you learn to work with the many yarn ends that result from all those color changes. Once you have a strong foundation with reversible intarsia, there are sixteen more squares to explore, featuring colorful quilt-, garden-, and space-inspired graphics.

The stitches that make this technique successful necessitated the development of a new language of crochet terminology. The Special Stitches section (page 10) includes tutorials for all of these stitches as well as basic guidelines for making color changes (page 136). In addition, each of the first twelve square patterns includes a list of the special stitches you'll need for that particular square, along with helpful notes and reminders.

You'll also find handy stitch diagrams throughout the book that use the standard symbols for half double crochet, double crochet, increases, and decreases. The diagrams use different colors to indicate when to make a color change and whether that change should be at the end of a stitch, after the stitch, or right in the middle of the stitch. The diagrams will be very helpful as a visual "plan" to help you keep track of the color changes as you work.

Although I've included ten afghan patterns to use the squares you create, there are infinite possibilities for combining squares and using your own favorite colors. I hope you'll enjoy not only learning the technique, but also gaining the knowledge to create your own designs!

Tools and Materials

Here are some tips for choosing the right materials to get the best results from your colorwork.

HOOKS AND OTHER TOOLS

The great thing about crochet is that all you really need is a hook and some yarn. However, I've also found a number of handy little helper-tools to go along with the basics.

Hooks: A gauge swatch, as described in each afghan pattern, will help you determine which hook to use for each project. You may need to adjust your hook size in order to get the gauge indicated. Use a larger hook if your swatch is smaller than the indicated swatch size or a smaller hook if your swatch is larger than the indicated swatch size.

On the other hand, because all of the full-size projects are afghans, the finished dimensions may not be as important to you as the colorwork effect. The smoothness of the lines between your color changes can be affected by the size of hook you are using. A smaller hook will create tighter spaces between the loops of your stitches, making for smoother lines in your pattern. But, the tighter stitches will also make the fabric denser, so you have to find a balance. All of the patterns in this book are worked in squares that are thirty-six stitches wide, so it's easy to swatch the first few rows of the square with the hook size you have determined from your gauge swatch. You can then make adjustments to get the finished look that you want.

Stitch Markers: Stitch markers are helpful in the finishing and joining stages of the pattern.

- When joining squares or strips of squares, you can mark the center and beginning of each square beforehand to be sure that the rows and stitches are lining up as you stitch them together.

- When edging squares or strips, mark the same center and beginning of each square. You can use those markers to keep your edge stitches evenly distributed as you work into them.

Scissors: You may want to have a small pair attached to your workbag or worn around your neck for snipping ends as you work. A larger, sharper pair is better for trimming final ends after weaving in.

Needles: You will need a large-eyed needle for weaving in all of those yarn ends. A typical "yarn" needle is appropriate for thicker yarns; smaller "tapestry" needles can be used for finer yarns. The important thing is that the tip is blunt so you don't pierce the strands of yarn as you are weaving in ends.

Row Counter: A row or stitch counter can be very useful for keeping track of which row you are working on in the pattern. With so many color changes, it can be challenging to keep track without a counting system.

Yarn Holders: With most crochet, you are working with just one or two balls of yarn at a time. However, with reversible intarsia, you will often be working with multiple colors at once, and you'll touch each ball of yarn nearly every time you change colors. If you don't protect the larger balls

YARN HOLDERS

of yarn, the outer yarn may get worn from so much handling before you get around to using it.

I found several useful little bags and cozies for protecting yarn

- Small zipper or drawstring bags are great for protecting smaller center-pull balls or skeins of yarn.

- A sock-like "yarn cozy" can be great to hold medium to large balls. The cozy can stretch to fit a full skein and shrink to fit as the skein gets smaller.

YARN CHOICE

The yarn you choose for a certain project will depend on a number of factors, including your desired afghan size, the definition you would like between color changes, and the intended recipient. You'll also want to consider whether a certain yarn will hold and hide ends well (for example, a slippery silk yarn may allow ends to come loose).

Fiber

A variety of fibers are used in the ten sample afghans in this book, including wools, cottons, and acrylics. I tried to stick with washable yarns, superwash wools, and acrylic or cotton blends. Who wants an afghan that is going to shrink and felt up the first time

someone "helpfully" throws it in the washing machine? Some yarns were easier to work with than others, but they all created beautiful intarsia patterns. You may want to experiment with some different fiber contents to learn how they behave and what you like.

When selecting yarn for an intarsia project, keep in mind that you will have many yarn ends to weave in. Certain yarns are easier to weave in than others. Fluffier wool yarns (such as those used in Tyler's Space Adventure) may be easier to hide the ends in than stringier cotton-blend yarns (such as those used in A World Too Wide). However, with careful handling, any yarn can be used. Check out Weaving In Ends on page 132 for help with cutting down on the number of ends and for tips on hiding them.

Weight

Various weights of yarn can be used for any of the projects in this book by simply adjusting the hook size to match the yarn. The squares will be smaller if you use a sportweight yarn for a project that calls for worsted or chunky weight, so you can either make more squares or plan to make a smaller blanket. Refer to a project that uses a similar yarn to the one you chose to help you determine the appropriate hook size. Make sure you don't skip reading the Notes in the project for any instructions related to the yarn weight.

Note that several of these afghans are worked in a chunky-weight yarn. Although reversible intarsia stitches look good in a #5 chunky-weight yarn, I don't recommend using a #6 bulky-weight yarn. The details of the images and shapes lose definition when worked in a yarn that is too thick.

Special Stitches

This section includes the special stitches that will be used to create reversible colorwork. Each of the twelve learning square patterns will refer you to the specific stitches you'll need.

REVERSIBLE COLOR CHANGE GUIDELINES

Half Double Crochet (hdc)
- Don't carry a new color before upright color changes.
- Carry a new color under the last stitch before angled color changes (under both stitches of an increase or second stitch of a decrease).
- Always flip the yarn up after a color change (unless a late color change is indicated).
- Use "flat decreases" (hdc-sc-tog) rather than hdc2tog.
- Late color changes are only used with hdc stitches.

Double Crochet (dc)
- Always carry a new color under the last stitch before a color change (under both stitches of an increase or second stitch of a decrease).
- Carry a new color under the last stitch before a half-color dc that will use that color for the bottom half.

When to Carry Yarn
- Only along the top of or underneath *same* color stitches.
- Under the last stitch before *any* dc or angled hdc.

REVERSIBLE INTARSIA SPECIAL STITCHES

Reversible Color Change (change to):
Work indicated st to last yo of the st in prev color, yo with new color **(Figure 1)**, and pull through all loops on hook, flip prev color yarnover to back of work between hook and yarn **(Figure 2)**, leaving prev color at top of back of work to be picked up on next row **(Figure 3)**.

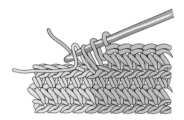

Figure 1

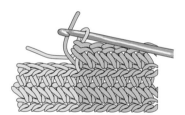

Figure 2

Figure 3

Double Crochet Reversible Color Change (change to):
Carry new color under last st in prev color **(Figure 1)**. With prev color, work final dc to last yo of st **(Figure 2)**, pull new color yarn to hide carried yarn in st, yo with new color and pull through 2 lps on hook, flip prev color yarn **(Figure 3)** over to back of work between hook and yarn, leaving it ready to pick up on the next row **(Figure 4)**.

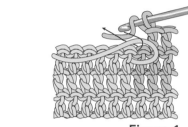

Figure 1

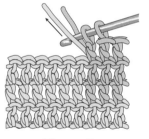

Figure 2

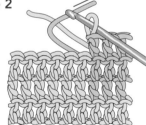

Figure 3

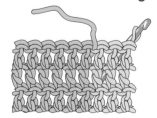

Figure 4

Late Color Change (late change to):

Work up to last st of same color **(Figure 1)**. Carry new color under last hdc in prev color **(Figure 2)**. Still with prev color, yo, pull through all loops **(Figure 3)**. Pull new color tight to hide under st(s) just made. Drop prev color behind work, pick up new color, complete next hdc with new color. Continue working in new color, leaving first color ready to pick up on next row **(Figure 4)**. Find Tips and Tricks for Working Late Color Changes on page 32.

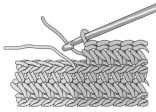

Figure 1

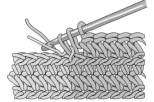

Figure 2

Figure 3

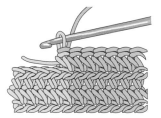

Figure 4

Hdc-sc decrease (hdc-sc-tog):

Yo, insert hook into next st, yo, pull up lp, insert hook into next st, yo, pull up lp **(4 lps on hook; Figure 1)**, yo, pull through all 4 lps. When changing colors, you will join new color in last yo of dec and flip dropped yarn up between hook and new yarn before working next st **(Figure 2)**.

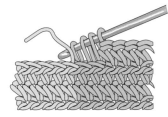

Figure 1

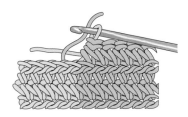

Figure 2

Hdc-sc-hdc decrease (hdc-sc-hdc-tog):

Yo, insert hook in next st, pull up lp, insert hook in next st, pull up lp, yo,insert hook in next st, pull up lp, yo and draw through all 6 lps.

Double Crochet Decrease (dc2tog) Color Change:

Work dc2tog to final yo, yo with new color **(Figure 1)**, and complete st. Flip prev color yarn up between hook and new yarn **(Figure 2)**. Work next inc under strand of new color and in last prev color st **(Figure 3)**.

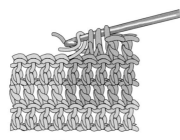

Figure 1

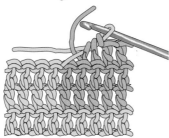

Figure 2

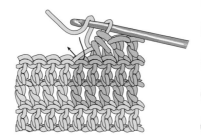

Figure 3

Double Crochet Increase Color Change (2 dc in st before change to):

Carry new color under 2 dc in indicated st up to last yo of second dc **(Figure 1)**. Pull new color tight to hide under sts **(Figure 2)** before yo with new color to complete inc. Flip yarn up between hook and new yarn **(Figure 3)**.

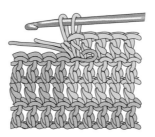

Figure 1

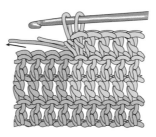

Figure 2

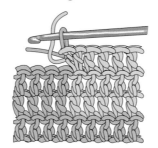

Figure 3

Half-Color Double Crochet (½-color dc A/B or colors indicated for top/bottom):

Drop top color (same as lp on hook) to back of work. With bottom color, yo, insert hook into next st **(Figure 1)**, yo, pull up lp, drop bottom color to back of work. With top color (yo **(Figure 2)**, pull through 2 bottom-color lps **(Figure 3)**, yo, pull through 2 top-color lps. For color change after ½-color dc, bring up bottom color on last yo and flip top color over to back of work as usual.

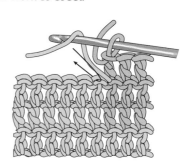

Figure 1

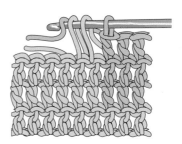

Figure 2

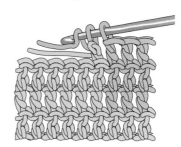

Figure 3

Reverse Half-Color Double Crochet Stitch (rev½-color dc):

Do not flip yarn after color change before a rev½-color dc. Drop top color to back of piece, work bottom half of st under strand of top color **(Figure 1)**. With bottom color, yo, insert hook into next st **(Figure 2)**, yo, pull up lp **(Figure 3)**. With top color, yo, bringing yarn up over top of yarn strand, pull through 2 bottom color lps **(Figure 4)**, with top color above strand, yo, pull through 2 top color lps **(Figure 5)**. Next dc will be worked with top color under strand and next st **(Figure 6)**.

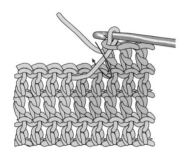

Figure 1

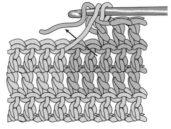

Figure 2

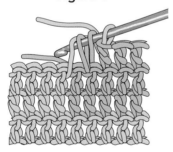

Figure 3

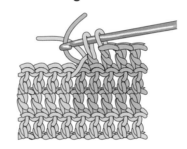

Figure 4

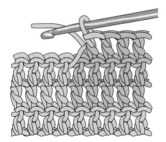

Figure 5

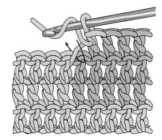

Figure 6

Reading Stitch Diagrams

The typical grid-type color charts used in most crocheted colorwork are not as useful in reversible intarsia. Stitch-symbol diagrams are much more helpful because the symbols can indicate where to use the late color changes, increases, and decreases that create the smooth lines in this technique. If you are familiar with reading stitch diagrams, you should have no problem understanding the diagrams in this book, though there are a few minor differences to watch for:

Always start at the lower right of a stitch diagram. Whether you are right-handed or left-handed, you will begin following the pattern from the same point.

Stitch count numbers indicate the number of plain hdc or dc stitches you will work in that color before the next color change, increase, or decrease. Be careful to note if the color change is a regular change or a late change before completing the last stitch. Note that these numbers are different from the stitch counts at the ends of rows in the written text (See Pattern Notes for All Squares on page 16).

Late Color Changes are indicted by a different color on the top bar of the stitch symbol. If you find yourself missing the late changes, it may help to circle each one before you begin.

Half-Color Double Crochets are indicated when the top half of the symbol is one color and the bottom half is another.

Reverse Half-Color Double Crochets are indicated in the same way as the half-color double crochets, with the top half one color and the bottom another. Just remember to follow the instructions for a rev ½-color dc any time the new color yarn strand is coming toward your hook, rather than already under it.

When joining a new color that will be joined to a larger section of the same color, make sure to note which direction the stitches will be coming from on the first row of the join. This will tell you which section of color needs a larger ball of yarn. See Yarn Preparation on page 132.

CROCHET SYMBOL KEY

○	= chain (ch)
T ╱	= half double crochet (hdc)
T	= late color change indicated by different colored horizontal bar
⋁ or V	= 2 hdc in same stitch
⋏ or ⋏	= half double crochet - single crochet together (hdc-sc-tog)
⋎	= 3 hdc in same stitch
⋏	= hdc-sc-hdc-tog
⊤	= double crochet
⊤	= ½-color dc or rev½-color dc depending on direction of work
⊬ or ⊬	= 2 dc in same stitch
⋏ or ⋏	= 2 dc together (2dctog)
⋓	= 3 dc in same stitch
⋏	= 3 dc together (3dctog)

CHAPTER 2
Learning and "Quilt" Squares

Basic Techniques and Geometric Squares

The geometric and quilt-inspired squares in this chapter are designed to help you learn all of the various stitches used in the reversible intarsia technique. Each group of four squares focuses on a particular aspect of the technique, with three "learning" squares followed by one quilt square that uses the stitches learned in that section. The final group of four squares (#13–16) are all inspired by traditional quilt-square patterns, combining everything you've learned in the earlier sections.

Yarn

Worsted weight (#4 Medium).

Shown Here: Berroco Comfort (50% super fine nylon, 50% super fine acrylic; 210 yd [193 m]/3.5 oz [100 g])

Color A: #9759 Duck Teal

Color B: #9717 Raspberry Coulis

Color C: #9740 Seedling (light green)

Color D: #9727 Spanish Brown

Color E: #9780 Dried Plum

(See Afghan Layouts for quantities for individual projects or estimate about 2 squares per 100 g ball.)

Hook

H/8 (5.0 mm) or hook needed to obtain gauge.

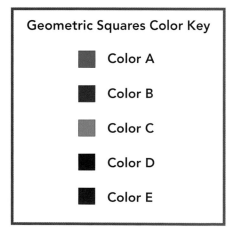

Geometric Squares Color Key

- ■ Color A
- ■ Color B
- ■ Color C
- ■ Color D
- ■ Color E

Notions

Size 16 tapestry or yarn needle; scissors.

Gauge

14 hdc × 12 rows = 4" × 4" (10 × 10 cm); 14 dc × 9 rows = 4" × 4" (10 × 10 cm).

Finished Size

Each square measures about 10" × 10" (25.5 × 25.5 cm), including 2 rounds of single crochet edging.

Information for All Squares

Read through the following information before moving on to the squares, to ensure that you have all of the necessary details to create clean, beautiful squares!

PATTERN NOTES FOR ALL SQUARES:

- Begin each row with ch 1, pull up loop on hook to height of next stitch, do not skip first stitch. This creates smoother edges for joining squares.
- Always begin a new ball or bobbin of yarn when you begin a new color (see Joining a New Color on page 136), unless you can carry the yarn above or below stitches of the same color (see When to Carry Yarn on page 134).
- Each time you work the first stitch in a new color, give the yarn you just dropped a gentle tug to tighten the loop.
- After completing all of the stitches in a given color, cut off yarns, leaving 4–6" (10–15 cm) to weave in under stitches of the same color (see Weaving In Ends on page 132).
- Stitch counts in pattern text indicate the number of stitches of each color at the top of each row, which may be different than the number of stitches worked if you are doing late color changes.
- On stitch diagrams, the numbers indicate how many plain hdc or dc stitches you will work in that color before the next color change, increase, or decrease.
- Always start reading a stitch diagram at the lower left (whether you are right-handed or left-handed).
- See Reading Stitch Diagrams on page 14 for more information.

EDGING ON ALL SQUARES

Turn work after last row. Join with sl st in last stitch made.

RND 1: Ch 1, sc in each st across to last st of last row, [3 sc in corner, rotate square to work next side, work 34 sc evenly spaced across to next corner] 3 times, 2 sc in corner, join with sl st to first sc—148 sc.

RND 2: Ch 1, [sc in next 36 sc, 3 sc in next sc] 4 times, join with sl st to first sc—156 sc.

Finish off.

Note: See individual afghan layouts in Section 3 to determine whether or not squares for a certain project need edging.

Tips for Edging Squares

- For smoother edges when working into sides of stitches, insert hook under just 2 loops of the side stitches rather than in larger holes between stitches.

- Because the finished work is completely reversible, left-handed crocheters can get the exact same image as right-handers by not turning the square after the last row and working the edging on the opposite side of the work.

- If you will be sewing squares together rather than crocheting them together, leave 2–3 feet (61–91.5 cm) of yarn after finishing off the square.

PART 1:
Reversible Color Changes in Upright Stitches

You will begin by learning how to work the Reversible Color Change in basic half double and double crochet stitches. Each square in Part 1 will add one new color to ease you into working with multiple yarn balls while you practice creating upright stitches. You will see some instructions in italics in the first twelve "learning squares" to help you learn when to carry yarn, join a new ball of yarn, or to call attention to other helpful reminders. These instructions will not be included in later squares.

Four Square

Half Double Crochet with Two Colors

The majority of crochet colorwork is done in single crochet, but reversible intarsia was designed specifically to work with the taller half double and double crochet stitches. This makes projects faster to work up and creates a softer fabric that is perfect for afghans, scarves, and anything else that requires a smooth drape. In this square, you'll be working with just two balls of yarn. In subsequent squares, you'll ease into working with more yarn balls (especially helpful if you're new to colorwork).

Notes

- See Pattern Notes for All Squares (on page 16).
- Refer to Special Stitches: Reversible Color Change
- Refer to Stitch Diagram 1 on page 19 for assistance.

Pattern

With B, ch 18, attach A (see Multicolor Beginning Chain on page 136), ch 19—37 ch.

ROW 1: Hdc in second ch from hook and next 17 ch, change to B, hdc in next 18 ch, turn—18 A, 18 B (36 hdc).

ROW 2: Ch 1, hdc in first 18 hdc, change to A, hdc in next 18 hdc, turn—18 B, 18 A.

ROW 3: Ch 1, hdc in first 18 hdc, change to B, hdc in next 18 hdc, turn—18 A, 18 B.

ROWS 4–15: Rep Rows 2 and 3. At end of last row, change to C, and *cut off colors A and B.*

ROW 16: Ch 1, hdc in next 18 hdc, change to D, hdc in next 18 hdc, turn—18 C, 18 D.

ROW 17: Ch 1, hdc in next 18 hdc, change to C, hdc in next 18 hdc, turn—18 D, 18 C.

ROWS 18–30: Rep Rows 16 and 17. Fasten off all colors and weave in ends under stitches of the same color.

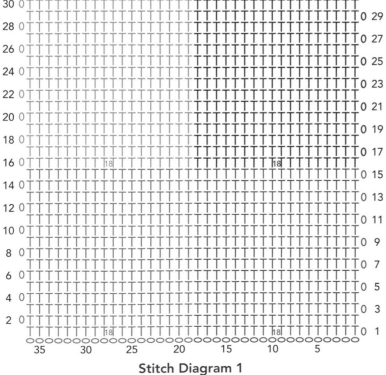

Stitch Diagram 1

The Yarn Flip

One of the key differences that distinguish reversible intarsia from other crocheted colorwork is the yarn flip (see **Figure 27** on page 137), which is done after each color change. By bringing the yarn up in between the hook and new yarn, you avoid the vertical stranding typically seen on the wrong side of the work. These strands are hidden inside the first stitch of the new color and brought to the top of the stitch, ready to be picked up on the following row. After completing the first stitch in the new color, remember to give the old color a gentle tug to tighten the yarn for a smoother look between color changes.

Nine-Patch

Half Double Crochet with Three Colors

In this square, you'll be working with three colors at the same time. As long as you remember to untangle your yarns at least every few rows, you should be able to avoid creating a tangled mess. This square is the first and simplest of the squares that were directly inspired by traditional quilt patterns. A similar design is often used as a "setting" block between more complicated blocks in a quilt.

Notes

- See Pattern Notes for All Squares (on page 16).
- Refer to Special Stitches: Reversible Color Change.
- Refer to Stitch Diagram 2 on page 21 for assistance.

Pattern

With D, ch 12, attach B, ch 12, *attach new ball D*, ch 13—37 ch.

ROW 1: Hdc in second ch from hook and next 11 ch, change to B, hdc in next 12 ch, change to D, hdc across, turn—12 D, 12 B, 12 D (36 hdc).

ROW 2: Ch 1, hdc in first 12 hdc, change to B, hdc in next 12 hdc, change to D, hdc across, turn—12 D, 12 B, 12 D.

ROWS 3–10: Rep Row 2. At end of last row, change to *new ball B,* and *cut off both D balls.*

ROW 11: Ch 1, hdc in first 12 hdc, change to C, *carry B under* hdc in next 12 hdc, change to B, hdc across, turn—12 B, 12 A, 12 B.

ROW 12: Ch 1, hdc in first 12 hdc, change to C, hdc in next 12 hdc, change to B, hdc across, turn—12 B, 12 A, 12 B.

ROWS 13–20: Rep Row 12. At end of last row, change to *new ball D.*

ROW 21: Ch 1, *carry B under* hdc in first 12 hdc, change to B, hdc in next 12 hdc, change to *new ball D,* hdc across, turn—12 D, 12 B, 12 D.

ROW 22: Ch 1, hdc in first 12 hdc, change to B, hdc in next 12 hdc, change to D, hdc across, turn—12 D, 12 B, 12 D.

ROWS 23–30: Rep Row 22. Fasten off all colors and weave in ends.

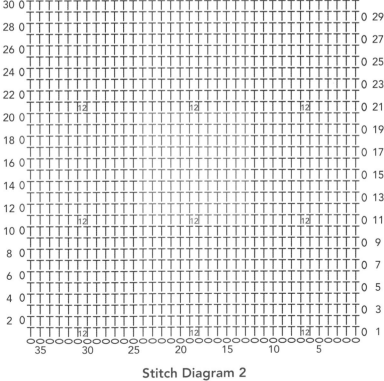

Stitch Diagram 2

Tips for Keeping Yarn Untangled

Every time you change colors, try to untangle the new color from all of the others and bring the entire ball forward and over the top of your work as you flip the previous color to the back of the work.

Keep the outer end of your balls or bobbins wrapped very tightly so that you have to pull the yarn out of the ball. This keeps the balls closer to your work, allowing for less yarn to get tangled (see Yarn Preparation on page 132).

Step Up

Double Crochet with Four Colors

The double crochet stitches used in this square are taller than the stitches used in previous squares, so the reversible color changes are slightly different. You will always carry the yarn you are about to pick up under the stitch before a color change, flipping the yarn up after the last instruction to "yarnover pull through two loops." Carrying the yarn brings it up into the stitch where it is easier to pick up without stranding.

Notes

- See Pattern Notes for All Squares on page 16.

- Before color changes, carry new color yarn under last dc in previous color. Pull new color tight to hide under stitches, before working final yarnover of last dc in new color.

- Italics are used to indicate all other times it is necessary to carry yarn before a color change.

- Remember to flip the previous yarn up after each color change, before beginning the first stitch in a new color.

- Refer to Special Stitches: Double Crochet Reversible Color Change (change to).

- Refer to Stitch Diagram 3 on page 23 for assistance.

Pattern

With D, ch 9, attach C, ch 9, attach B, ch 9, attach A, ch 11—38 ch.

ROW 1: Dc in third ch from hook and next 8 ch, change to B, dc in next 9 ch, change to C, dc in next 9 ch, change to D, dc across, turn—9 A, 9 B, 9 C, 9 D (36 dc).

ROW 2: Ch 1, dc in first 9 dc, change to C, dc in next 9 dc, change to B, dc in next 9 dc, change to A, dc across, turn—9 D, 9 C, 9 B, 9 A.

ROW 3: Ch 1, dc in first 9 dc, change to B, dc in next 9 dc, change to C, dc in next 9 dc, change to D, dc across, turn—9 A, 9 B, 9 C, 9 D.

ROWS 4–11: Rep Rows 2 and 3. *Cut off A and then change to A at end of last row.*

ROW 12: Ch 1, *carry D under* dc in first 9 dc, change to D, *carry C under* dc in next 9 dc, change to C, *carry B under* dc in next 9 dc, change to B, dc across, turn—9 A, 9 D, 9 C, 9 B.

ROW 13: Ch 1, dc in first 9 dc, change to C, dc in next 9 dc, change to D, dc in next 9 dc, change to A, dc across, turn—9 B, 9 C, 9 D, 9 A.

ROW 14: Ch 1, dc in first 9 dc, change to D, dc in next 9 dc, change to C, dc in next 9 dc, change to B, dc across, turn—9 A, 9 D, 9 C, 9 B.

ROWS 15–22: Rep Rows 13 and 14. Fasten off all colors and weave in ends.

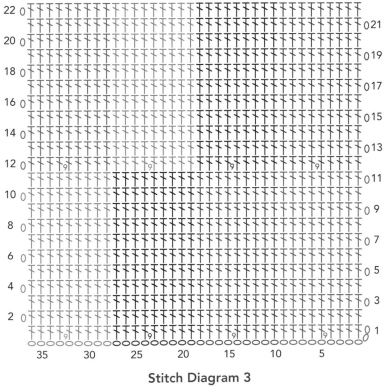

Stitch Diagram 3

The numbers along the diagram's axes read: 22, 20, 18, 16, 14, 12, 10, 8, 6, 4, 2 (left side); 21, 19, 17, 15, 13, 11, 9, 7, 5, 3, 1 (right side); 35, 30, 25, 20, 15, 10, 5 (bottom).

Have you ever tried tapestry crochet?

If you are not familiar with tapestry crochet, it is a traditional type of crocheted colorwork where unused colors are carried along underneath the stitches as you work them. When you are ready to use one of the other colors, you simply drop the color you have been using and yarn over with the next color you want to use. This creates a reversible fabric; however, the carried colors tend to peek out between the stitches, especially when worked in taller half double and double crochet stitches.

In the reversible intarsia technique, carrying the new color under the stitch just before a color change brings the new color up into the stitch you are working, in the same position as it would be in tapestry crochet, making it easier to pick up. As long as you remember to pull the new color tight under the stitch before using it, most of that carried yarn will be hidden under the stitch in the previous color.

Log Cabin

Quilt Square

Though the log cabin pattern has long been very popular among quilters, there are also various crocheted and knitted versions. To build the log cabin design, you usually start from the center square and build onto it by adding strips to each side so that it grows from the center out. With reversible intarsia crochet, you can create the same effect by working back and forth in rows, using only the upright color-change stitches you learned in the previous square.

Notes

- See Pattern Notes for All Squares on page 16.

- Before color changes, carry new color yarn under last dc in previous color. Pull new color tight to hide under stitches, before working final yarnover of last dc in new color.

- Remember to flip the previous yarn up after each color change, before beginning the first stitch in a new color.

- Refer to Special Stitches: Double Crochet Reversible Color Change (change to).

- Refer to Stitch Diagram 4 on page 25 for assistance.

Pattern

With D, ch 7, attach C, ch 31—38 ch.

ROW 1: Dc in third ch from hook and next 28 ch, change to D, dc across, turn—29 C, 7 D (36 dc).

ROW 2: Ch 1, dc in first 7 dc, change to C, dc across, turn—7 D, 29 C.

ROW 3: Ch 1, dc in first 29 dc, change to D, dc across, turn—29 C, 7 D.

ROW 4: Rep Row 2.

ROW 5: Ch 1, dc in first 7 dc, change to A, dc in next 15 dc, change to B, dc in next 7 dc, change to D, dc across, turn—7 C, 15 A, 7 B, 7 D.

ROW 6: Ch 1, dc in first 7 dc, change to B, dc in next 7 dc, change to A, dc in next 15 dc, change to C, dc across, turn—7 D, 7 B, 15 A, 7 C.

ROWS 7 AND 8: Rep Rows 5 and 6.

ROW 9: Ch 1, dc in first 7 dc, change to A, dc in next 7 dc, change to E, dc in next 8 dc, change to B, dc in next 7 dc, change to D, dc across, turn—7 C, 7 A, 8 E, 7 B, 7 D.

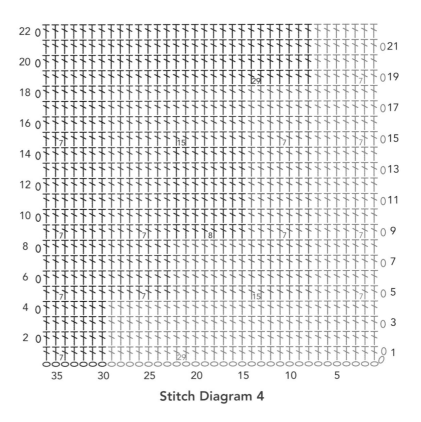

ROW 10: Ch 1, dc in first 7 dc, change to B, dc in next 7 dc, change to E, dc in next 8 dc, change to A, dc in next 7 dc, change to C, dc across, turn—7 D, 7 B, 8 E, 7 A, 7 C.

ROWS 11–14: Rep Rows 9 and 10.

ROW 15: Ch 1, dc in first 7 dc, change to A, dc in next 7 dc, change to B, dc in next 15 dc, change to D, dc across, turn—7 C, 7 A, 15 B, 7 D.

ROW 16: Ch 1, dc in first 7 dc, change to B, dc in next 15 dc, change to A, dc in next 7 dc, change to C, dc across, turn—7 D, 15 B, 7 A, 7 C.

ROWS 17 AND 18: Rep Rows 15 and 16.

ROW 19: Ch 1, dc in first 7 dc, change to D, dc across, turn—7 C, 29 D.

ROW 20: Ch 1, dc in first 29 dc, change to C, dc across, turn—29 D, 7 C.

ROWS 21 AND 22: Rep Rows 19 and 20. Fasten off all colors and weave in ends.

Stitch Diagram 4

PART 2:
Shaping Angles
with Half Double Crochet

If you have completed the squares in Part 1, you've learned upright reversible intarsia color changes in both half double and double crochet stitches. In Part 2, you'll explore a variety of designs using half double crochet stitches and learn to use late color changes, increases, and decreases to create a variety of angles.

SQUARE 5

Diagonal Stripes

Late Color Changes for Slow Angles

This square uses the natural slope of the stitches to create diagonal stripes. Although most crochet patterns will instruct you to change colors in the last yarnover of the final stitch in the previous color, in reversible intarsia you'll sometimes complete the last stitch and change colors on the first yarnover of the next stitch. These late color changes keep the first color on top of the next stitch, ready to be worked with the same color on the following row, creating smoother lines. By consistently working into the stitch to the same side of the previous stitch in that color, you can create very smooth angles.

Notes

- See Pattern Notes for All Squares on page 16.

- On increasing curves, always carry strands of the new color under the stitch worked just before the color change and gently pull the carried yarn to hide it under the stitches of the other color.

- As indicated in the pattern, on some angles, color change will be on the first yo of the first stitch (rather than the end of the last sc before a color change). This is so that the correct color loop is at the top of the stitch for the next row.

- Refer to Special Stitches: Reversible Color Change (change to) and Late Color Change (late change to).

- Refer to Stitch Diagram 5 on page 28 for assistance.

Pattern

With D, ch 5, attach C, ch 12, attach B, ch 12, attach A, ch 7—37 ch.

ROW 1: Hdc in second ch from hook and next 6 ch, change to B, hdc in next 12 ch, change to C, hdc in next 12 ch, change to D, hdc across, turn—7 A, 12 B, 12 C, 5 D (36 hdc).

ROW 2: Ch 1, hdc in each D-color hdc, late change to C, hdc in next 12 hdc, late change to B, hdc in next 12 hdc, late change to A, hdc across, turn.

ROW 3: Ch 1, hdc in each hdc to last A-color hdc, change to B, hdc in next 12 hdc, change to C, hdc in next 12 hdc, change to D, hdc across, turn.

ROWS 4–12: Alternate Rows 2 and 3.

ROW 13: Ch 1, hdc in first hdc, change to B, hdc in next 12 hdc, change to C, hdc in next 12 hdc, change to D, hdc across, turn—1 A, 12 B, 12 C, 11 D.

ROW 14: Ch 1, hdc in first 11 hdc, late change to C, hdc in next 12 hdc, late change to B, hdc in next 12 hdc, late change to A, hdc in last hdc, change to B, turn—12 D, 12 C, 12 B.

ROW 15: Ch 1, hdc in first 12 hdc, change to C, hdc in next 12 hdc, change to D, hdc across, turn—12 B, 12 C, 12 D.

ROW 16: Ch 1, hdc in first 12 hdc, late change to C, hdc in next 12 hdc, late change to B, hdc across, turn—13 D, 12 C, 11 B.

ROW 17: Ch 1, hdc in first 11 hdc, change to C, hdc in next 12 hdc, change to D, hdc in next 12 hdc, change to A, hdc in last hdc, turn—11 B, 12 C, 12 D, 1 A.

ROW 18: Ch 1, hdc in first hdc, late change to D, hdc in next 12 hdc, late change to C, hdc in next 12 hdc, late change to B, hdc across, turn—2 A, 12 D, 12 C, 10 B.

ROW 19: Ch 1, hdc in each hdc to last B-color hdc, change to C, hdc in next 12 hdc, change to D, hdc in next 12 hdc, change to A, hdc across, turn.

ROW 20: Ch 1, hdc in each A-color hdc, late change to D, hdc in next 12 hdc, late change to C, hdc in next 12 hdc, late change to B, hdc across, turn.

ROWS 21–30: Alternate Rows 19 and 20. Finish off all colors and weave in ends.

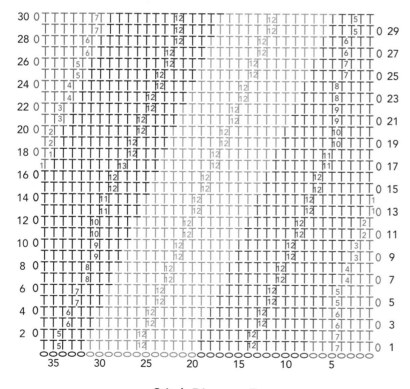

Stitch Diagram 5

SQUARE 6

Vertical Chevrons

Using Increases and Decreases

By alternating increases (two stitches worked in the same hdc) in one color with decreases (hdc-sc-tog) in the next color, you can create right angles. To continue those angles, you simply reverse the order (decrease, then increase) on every other row. An increase will always be paired with a decrease in order to maintain the same number of stitches at the end of each row. You'll also use late color changes to create smoother angles, as in the previous square.

Notes

- See Pattern Notes for All Squares on page 16.

- Always carry the strand of the new color under both stitches of an increase (2 hdc in the same stitch) worked just before a late color change followed by a decrease (hdc-sc-tog).

- Carry the strand of the new color under the second stitch of a decrease (hdc-sc-tog) followed by an increase.

- As indicated in the pattern, on some angles, color change will be on the first yo of the first stitch (rather than the end of the last st before a color change). This is so that the correct color loop is at the top of the stitch for the next row.

- Refer to Special Stitches: Reversible Color Change (change to), Late Color Change (late change to), Hdc-sc-decrease (hdc-sc-tog).

- Refer to Stitch Diagram 6 on page 30 for assistance.

Pattern

With B, ch 6, attach D, ch 9, attach C, ch 9, attach A, ch 13—37 ch.

ROW 1: Hdc in second ch from hook and next 9 ch, hdc-sc-tog, change to C, 2 hdc in next ch, hdc in next 6 ch, hdc-sc-tog, change to D, 2 hdc in next ch, hdc in next 6 ch, hdc-sc-tog, change to B, 2 hdc in next ch, hdc across, turn—11 A, 9 C, 9 D, 7 B (36 hdc).

ROW 2: Ch 1, hdc in each hdc to last B-color hdc, *carry D under* 2 hdc in next hdc, late change to D, hdc-sc-tog, hdc in next 6 hdc, *carry C under* 2 hdc in next hdc, late change to C, hdc-sc-tog, hdc in next 6 hdc, *carry A under* 2 hdc in next hdc, late change to A, hdc-sc-tog, hdc across, turn.

ROW 3: Ch 1, hdc in each hdc to last 2 A-color hdc, hdc-sc-tog, change to C, 2 hdc in next hdc, hdc in next 6 hdc, hdc-sc-tog, change to D, 2 hdc in next hdc, hdc in next 6 hdc, hdc-sc-tog, change to B, 2 hdc in next hdc, hdc across, turn.

ROWS 4 AND 5: Rep Rows 2 and 3.

ROW 6: Ch 1, hdc in first 11 hdc, *carry D under* hdc-sc-tog, change to D, 2 hdc in next hdc, hdc in next 6 hdc, *carry C under* hdc-sc-tog, change to C, 2 hdc in next hdc, hdc in next 6 hdc, *carry A under* hdc-sc-tog, change to A, 2 hdc in next hdc, hdc across, turn—12 B, 9 D, 9 C, 6 A.

ROW 7: Ch 1, hdc in each hdc to last A-color hdc, *carry C under* 2 hdc in next hdc, late change to C, hdc-sc-tog, hdc in next 6 hdc, *carry D under* 2 hdc in next hdc, late change to D, hdc-sc-tog, hdc in next 6 hdc, *carry B under* 2 hdc in next hdc, late change to B, hdc-sc-tog, hdc across, turn.

ROW 8: Ch 1, hdc in each hdc to last 2 B-color hdc, hdc-sc-tog, change to D, 2 hdc in next hdc, hdc in next 6 hdc, hdc-sc-tog, change to C, 2 hdc in next hdc, hdc in next 6 hdc, hdc-sc-tog, change to A, 2 hdc in next hdc, hdc across, turn.

ROWS 9 AND 10: Rep Rows 7 and 8.

ROW 11: Ch 1, hdc in first 10 hdc, *carry C under* hdc-sc-tog, change to C, 2 hdc in next hdc, hdc in next 6 hdc, *carry D under* hdc-sc-tog, change to D, 2 hdc in next hdc, hdc in next 6 hdc, *carry B under* hdc-sc-tog, change to B, 2 hdc in next hdc, hdc across, turn—11 A, 9 C, 9 D, 7 B.

ROWS 12–15: Rep Rows 2 and 3.

ROWS 16–20: Rep Rows 6–10.

ROWS 21–30: Rep Rows 11–20. Fasten off all colors and weave in ends.

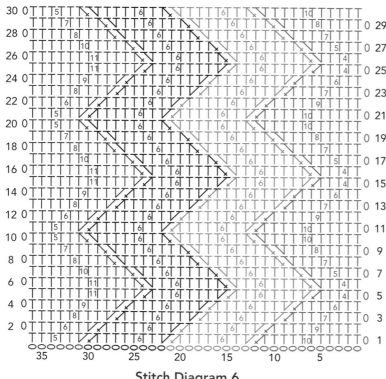

Stitch Diagram 6

Slopes

Every Other Stitch for Sharper Angles

This square builds on the angling skills learned in the previous two squares. This time, you'll be creating sharper angles by increasing and decreasing in every other stitch. The angles are not quite as smooth as those in Square 5, but by combining increases and decreases with late color changes, you can avoid the pixelated stair-step effect you see in typical single crochet colorwork.

Notes

- See Pattern Notes for All Squares on page 16.

- Although the increase and decrease stitches are the same as those in the previous two squares, you will need to carry the unused yarn more often to avoid stranding (leaving the unused color, exposed, along the back of the work).

- Always carry new color under last hdc of old color to bring it up into the stitch. Italics are used to indicate all other times it is necessary to carry yarn before a color change.

- On increasing curves, always carry strands of unused color under the stitches worked just before the color change and gently pull the carried yarn to hide it under the stitches of the other color.

- Refer to Special Stitches: Reversible Color Change (change to), Late Color Change (late change to), Hdc-sc-decrease (hdc-sc-tog).

- Refer to Stitch Diagram 7 on page 33 for assistance.

Pattern

With D, ch 17, attach A, ch 20—37 ch.

ROW 1: Hdc in second ch from hook and next 16 ch, hdc-sc-tog, change to D, 2 hdc in next ch, hdc across, turn—18 A, 18 D (36 hdc).

ROW 2: Ch 1, hdc in first 18 hdc, *carry A under previous hdc* and 2 hdc in next hdc, late change to A, hdc-sc-tog, hdc across, turn—21 D, 15 A.

ROW 3: Ch 1, hdc in first 12 hdc, hdc-sc-tog, change to D, *carry D under* 2 hdc in next hdc, hdc across, turn—13 A, 23 D.

ROW 4: Ch 1, hdc in first 23 hdc, *carry A under previous hdc* and 2 hdc in next hdc, late change to A, hdc-sc-tog, hdc across, turn—26 D, 10 A.

ROW 5: Ch 1, hdc in first 7 hdc, hdc-sc-tog, change to C, 2 hdc in next 2 hdc, late change to D, hdc-sc-tog, hdc across, turn—8 A, 5 C, 23 D.

ROW 6: Ch 1, hdc in first 20 hdc, hdc-sc-tog, change to C, *carry C under* 2 hdc in next hdc, hdc in next 5 hdc, *carry A under previous hdc* and 2 hdc in next hdc, late change to A, hdc-sc-tog, hdc across, change to C, turn—21 D, 10 C, 5 A.

STITCH GUIDE

hdc-sc-tog

Working the increase after decrease over every other stitch will work just a little differently than it does when worked over every stitch.

Increase after Decrease (hdc-sc-tog) On Sharper Angles:

Carry new color across unused st for Reversible Color Change and flip yarn up as usual (**Figure 1**). Yo, insert hook under carried strand and first st of new color (**Figure 2**), work 2 hdc in same sp (**Figure 3**). Working other direction, carry unused color under last hdc and 2 hdc in next hdc before color change (**Figure 4**). Pull carried yarn tight to hide under sts before using it for next st (**Figure 5**), work hdc-sc-tog in new color (**Figure 6**).

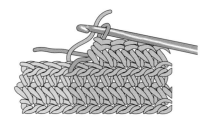

Figure 1

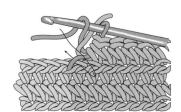

Figure 2

Figure 3

Figure 4

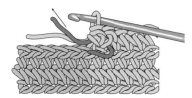

Figure 5

Figure 6

Tips and Tricks for Working Late Color Changes

Before starting each square, consider highlighting all instances of "late change to," to help you remember when to work them. If you don't want to mark up your book, try highlighter tape (found in many local yarn stores and office supply stores).

Remember that the stitch counts at the ends of some rows indicate the number of each color at the tops of your stitches, which does not necessarily equal the number of stitches worked in each color due to late color changes.

When working back into the tops of late color changes, be careful not to skip them. If you have pulled the dropped yarn too tight, it is easy to miss them when working the next row.

Because crochet stitches do not stack up right on top of one another, you are working with the angle of the stitches rather than against them.

ROW 7: Ch 1, hdc in first 15 hdc, *carry D under previous hdc* and 2 hdc in next hdc, late change to D, hdc-sc-tog, hdc across, turn—18 C, 18 D.

ROW 8: Ch 1, hdc in first 15 hdc, hdc-sc-tog, change to C, *carry C under* 2 hdc in next hdc, hdc across, turn—16 D, 20 C.

ROW 9: Ch 1, hdc in first 20 hdc, *carry D under previous hdc* and 2 hdc in next hdc, late change to D, hdc-sc-tog, hdc across, turn—23 C, 13 D.

ROW 10: Ch 1, hdc in first 10 hdc, hdc-sc-tog, change to C, *carry C under* 2 hdc in next hdc, hdc across, turn—11 D, 25 C.

ROW 11: Ch 1, hdc in first 22 hdc, hdc-sc-tog, change to B, *carry B under* 2 hdc in next 2 hdc, late change to D, hdc-sc-tog, hdc across, turn—23 C, 5 B, 8 D.

ROW 12: Ch 1, hdc in first 5 hdc, hdc-sc-tog, change to B, *carry B under* 2 hdc in next hdc, hdc in next 5 hdc, *carry C under previous hdc* and 2 hdc in next hdc, late change to C, hdc-sc-tog, hdc across, turn—6 D, 10 B, 20 C.

ROW 13: Ch 1, hdc in first 17 hdc, hdc-sc-tog, change to B, *carry B under* 2 hdc in next hdc, hdc across, turn—18 C, 18 B.

ROWS 14–16: Rep Rows 2–4 using colors B and C to replace D and A.

ROWS 17 AND 18: Rep Rows 5 and 6 using colors C, A, B to replace A, C, D.

ROWS 19–22: Rep Rows 7–10 using colors A and B to replace C and D.

ROWS 23 AND 24: Rep Rows 11 and 12 using colors A, D, B to replace D, C, B.

ROW 25: Rep Row 13 using colors A and D to replace C and B.

ROWS 26–30: Rep Rows 2–6. Fasten off all colors and weave in ends.

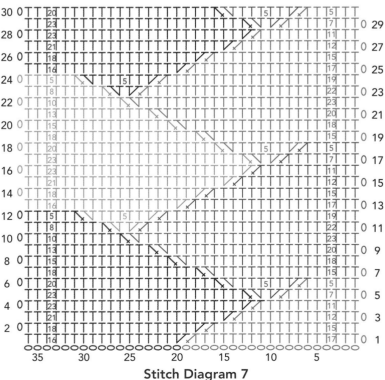

Stitch Diagram 7

Pinwheel

Quilt Square

The pinwheel is another common quilt-square motif that often contributes to more intricate designs when combined with other quilt squares. Although combining increases and decreases with late color changes creates almost-right angles, it is necessary to alternate between these sharper-angle stitches and simple late color changes to create the 45-degree angles we need to give the appearance of the pinwheel pattern.

Tip: Count Your Stitches

Don't forget to count your stitches at least every few rows. It's easy to add an extra stitch on an increase and forget to balance it with a decrease (keeping the same number of stitches on every row).

Notes

- See Pattern Notes for All Squares on page 16.

- Refer to Special Stitches: Reversible Color Change (change to); Late Color Change (late change to); Hdc-sc Decrease (hdc-sc-tog).

- Refer to Stitch Diagram 8 on page 35 for assistance.

Pattern

With C, ch 18, attach A, ch 18, attach B, ch 1 —37 ch.

ROW 1: Hdc in second ch from hook, late change to A, hdc-sc-tog in same ch as last hdc and next ch, hdc in next 16 ch, change to C, hdc in next 16 ch, hdc-sc-tog, change to D, hdc in same ch as last hdc, turn—2 B, 16 A, 17 C, 1 D (36 hdc).

ROW 2: Ch 1, 2 hdc in first hdc, late change to C, hdc-sc-tog, hdc in next 15 hdc, change to A, hdc in next 14 hdc, hdc-sc-tog, change to B, 2 hdc in next hdc, hdc in last hdc, turn— 3 D, 15 C, 15 A, 3 B.

ROW 3: Ch 1, hdc in each hdc to last B-color hdc, 2 hdc in next hdc, late change to A, hdc-sc-tog, hdc in each A-color hdc, change to C, hdc in each C-color hdc, change to D, hdc across, turn.

ROW 4: Ch 1, hdc in each hdc to last D-color hdc, 2 hdc in next hdc, late change to C, hdc-sc-tog, hdc in each C-color hdc, change to A, hdc in each A-color hdc, change to B, hdc across, turn.

ROW 5: Ch 1, hdc in each hdc to last B-color hdc, 2 hdc in next hdc, late change to A, hdc-sc-tog, hdc in each A-color hdc, change to C, hdc in each hdc to last 2 C-color hdc, hdc-sc-tog, change to D, 2 hdc in next hdc, hdc across, turn.

ROWS 6–10: Alternate Rows 4 and 3.

ROW 11: Rep Row 5—13 B, 5 A, 5 C, 13 D.

ROW 12: Ch 1, hdc in first 12 hdc, 2 hdc in first hdc, late change to C, hdc-sc-tog, hdc in next 3 hdc, change to A, hdc in next 3 hdc, hdc-sc-tog, change to B, 2 hdc in next hdc, hdc in last hdc, turn—15 D, 3 C, 4 A, 14 B.

ROW 13: Rep Row 5—16 B, 2 A, 2 C, 16 D.

ROW 14: Ch 1, hdc in first 16 hdc, late change to C, hdc in next 2 hdc, change to A, hdc-sc-tog, change to B, 2 hdc in next, hdc in last hdc, turn—17 D, 1 C, 1 A, 17 B.

ROW 15: Ch 1, hdc in first 17 hdc, late change to A, hdc in next hdc, change to C, hdc in next hdc, change to D, hdc across, change to B, turn—18 B, 1 C, 17 D.

ROW 16: Ch 1, hdc in first 16 hdc, hdc-sc-tog, change to A, hdc in same hdc as last hdc, change to C, hdc in next hdc, late change to D, hdc-sc-tog in same hdc as last hdc and next hdc, hdc across—17 B, 1 A, 2 C, 16 D.

ROW 17: Ch 1, hdc in first 16 hdc, change to C, hdc in next 2 hdc, change to A, 2 hdc in next hdc, late change to B, hdc-sc-tog, hdc across, turn—16 D, 2 C, 3 A, 15 B.

ROW 18: Ch 1, hdc in first 15 hdc, change to A, hdc in next 3 hdc, change to C, hdc in next hdc, 2 hdc in next hdc, late change to D, hdc-sc-tog, hdc across—15 B, 3 A, 4 C, 14 D.

ROW 19: Ch 1, hdc in first 14 hdc, change to C, hdc in next 4 hdc, change to A, hdc in next 2hdc, 2 hdc in next hdc, late change to B, hdc-sc-tog, hdc across, turn—14 D, 4 C, 5 A, 13 B.

ROW 20: Ch 1, hdc in each hdc to last 2 B-color hdc, hdc-sc-tog, change to A, 2 hdc in next hdc, hdc in each A-color hdc, change to C, hdc in each hdc to last C-color hdc, 2 hdc in next hdc, late change to D, hdc-sc-tog, hdc across, turn.

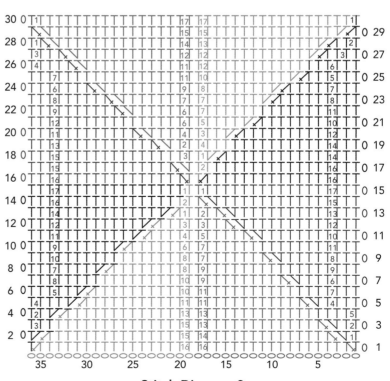

Stitch Diagram 8

ROW 21: Ch 1, hdc in each hdc to last 2 D-color hdc, hdc-sc-tog, change to C, 2 hdc in next hdc, hdc in each C-color hdc, change to A, hdc in each A-color hdc, late change to B, hdc across, turn.

ROW 22: Ch 1, hdc in each hdc to last 2 B-color hdc, hdc-sc-tog, change to A, 2 hdc in next hdc, hdc in each A-color hdc, change to C, hdc in each C-color hdc, late change to D, hdc across, turn.

ROW 23: Ch 1, hdc in each hdc to last 2 D-color hdc, hdc-sc-tog, change to C, 2 hdc in next hdc, hdc in each C-color hdc, change to A, hdc in each hdc to last A-color hdc, 2 hdc in next hdc, late change to B, hdc-sc-tog, hdc across, turn.

ROWS 24–27: Rep Rows 20–23.

ROW 28: Rep Row 20.

ROW 29: Ch 1, hdc-sc-tog, change to C, 2 hdc in next hdc, hdc in next 15 hdc, change to A, hdc in next 15 hdc, 2 hdc in next hdc, change to B, hdc-sc-tog, turn—1 D, 17 C, 17 A, 1 B.

ROW 30: Ch 1, hdc in first hdc, change to A, hdc in next 17 hdc, change to C, hdc in next 17 hdc, late change to D, hdc in last hdc— 1 B, 17 A, 18 C.

Notes for Left-Handed Crocheters

As a left-handed designer, I like to create fabric that is reversible so that the finished product will be the same on both sides, regardless of which hand you hold your hook in. All of the patterns in this book can be followed just as they are written, but here are a few notes for lefties to keep in mind when doing reversible intarsia:

- Row 1 of each square will be your wrong side (WS), whereas it would be the right side (RS) for a right-handed crocheter.

- Always start at the lower right of a stitch diagram. Whether you are left-handed or right-handed, you will begin following the first row from right to left, then every other row from left to right.

- Left-handed crocheters will end up with a mirror image of what is seen in the diagram, but because the finished work is completely reversible you can simply flip the work to the opposite side if you want your piece to look the same as the sample.

- Do not flip your work at the end of the last row of each square to keep the right side of the work facing you.

PART 3:
Shaping with Double Crochet

In Part 1, you learned how to work upright double crochet stitches using the yarn flip to avoid stranding. Now, you'll begin working with double crochet increases, decreases, and half-color stitches to create angles and shaping. Although you can create all sorts of simple shapes using the half double crochet stitches we have already learned, it can be challenging to follow a gridded color chart because those stitches are taller than they are wide. On the other hand, one row of double crochet is about equal in height to two rows of single crochet. The tops of each stitch and the bottoms can be counted as two rows on the grid, and adding increases and decreases can give smoother angles. So it is easier to produce much more detailed images by incorporating all of the stitches practiced in this section than you can get with most single or half double crochet colorwork patterns.

Diamonds

Double Crochet Diagonal

The simplest shaping worked in double crochet uses increases (two dc in one stitch) with decreases (dc2tog). This is very similar to using increases and decreases in half double crochet, except that late color changes are not used because they don't work as well with taller double crochet stitches as they do with the shorter half-double crochet stitches.

Notes

- See Pattern Notes for All Squares on page 16.

- You will need 2 balls of Colors A, B, and D, as well as 1 ball of Color C. Divide your skeins into smaller balls as necessary (see Yarn Preparation on page 132).

- Always carry new color under last dc of old color to bring it up into the stitch. Italics are used to indicate all other times it is necessary to carry yarn before a color change.

- Carry strand of new color under both stitches of an increase (2 dc in the same st) worked just before a decrease (dc2tog).

- Carry strand of the new color under only the second stitch of a decrease (dc2tog) followed by an increase.

- Refer to Special Stitches: Double Crochet Reversible Color Change (change to) and Double Crochet Decrease (dc2tog) Color Change.

- Refer to Stitch Diagram 9 on page 39 for assistance.

Pattern

With A, ch 8, attach B, ch 9, attach D, ch 2, attach B, ch 9, attach A, ch 10—38 ch.

ROW 1: Dc in third ch from hook and next 5 ch, dc2tog, change to B, 2 dc in next ch, dc in next 6 ch, dc2tog, change to D, 2 dc in next 2 ch, change to B, dc2tog, dc in next 6 ch, 2 dc in next ch, change to A, dc2tog, dc across, turn—7 A, 9 B, 4 D, 9 B, 7 A (36 dc).

ROWS 2–4: Ch 1, dc in each dc to last 3 A-color dc, dc2tog, change to B, 2 dc in next dc, dc in next 6 dc, dc2tog, change to D, 2 dc in next dc, dc in each dc to last D-color dc, *carry B under* 2 dc in next dc, change to B, dc2tog, dc in next 6 dc, *carry D under* 2 dc in next dc, change to A, dc2tog, dc across, turn.

ROW 5: Ch 1, dc2tog, change to B, 2 dc in next dc, dc in next 6 dc, dc2tog, change to D, 2 dc in next dc, dc in next 12 dc, *carry B under* 2 dc in next dc, change to B, dc2tog, dc in next 6 dc, *carry A under* 2 dc in next dc, change to A, dc2tog, turn—1 A, 9 B, 16 D, 9 B, 1 A.

ROW 6: Ch 1, change to B, dc in first 7 dc, dc2tog, change to D, 2 dc in next dc, dc in next 15 dc, *carry B under* 2 dc in next dc, change to B, dc2tog, dc across, turn—8 B, 19 D, 9 B.

ROW 7: Ch 1, dc in first 6 dc, dc2tog, change to D, 2 dc in next dc, dc in next 6 dc, dc2tog, change to C, *carry D under* 2 dc in next 2 dc, change to D, dc2tog, dc in next 6 dc, *carry B under* 2 dc in next dc, change to B, dc2tog, dc across, turn—7 B, 9 D, 4 C, 9 D, 7 B.

ROWS 8–10: Ch 1, dc in each dc to last 3 B-color dc, dc2tog, change to D, 2 dc in next dc, dc in next 6 dc, dc2tog, change to C, 2 dc in next dc, dc in each dc to last C-color dc, *carry D under* 2 dc in next dc, change to D, dc2tog, dc in next 6 dc, *carry B under* 2 dc in next dc, change to B, dc2tog, dc across, turn.

ROW 11: Ch 1, dc2tog, change to D, 2 dc in next dc, dc in next 6 dc, dc2tog, change to C, 2 dc in next dc, dc in next 12 dc, *carry D under* 2 dc in next dc, change to D, dc2tog, dc in next 6 dc, *carry B under* 2 dc in next dc, change to B, dc2tog, turn—1 B, 9 D, 16 C, 9 D, 1 B.

ROW 12: Ch 1, 2 dc in next dc, change to D, dc2tog, dc in next 6 dc, 2 dc in next dc, change to C, dc2tog, dc in next 12 dc, *carry B under second st* as you work next dc2tog, change to D, 2 dc in next dc, dc in next 6 dc, *carry B under second st* as you work next dc2tog, change to B, 2 dc in last dc, turn—2 B, 9 D, 14 C, 9 D, 2 B.

ROWS 13–15: Ch 1, dc in each dc to last B-color dc, *carry D under* 2 dc in next dc, change to D, dc2tog, dc in next 6 dc, *carry C under* 2 dc in next dc, change to C, dc2tog, dc in each dc to last 3 C-color dc, dc2tog, change to D, 2 dc in next dc, dc in next 6 dc, dc2tog, change to B, 2 dc in next dc, dc across, turn.

ROW 16: Ch 1, dc in first 6 dc, *carry D under* 2 dc in next dc, change to D, dc2tog, dc in next 6 dc, *carry C under* 2 dc in next dc, change to C, 2 dc2tog, change to D, 2 dc in next dc, dc in next 6 dc, dc2tog, change to B, 2 dc in next dc, dc across, turn—8 B, 9 D, 2 C, 9 C, 8 B.

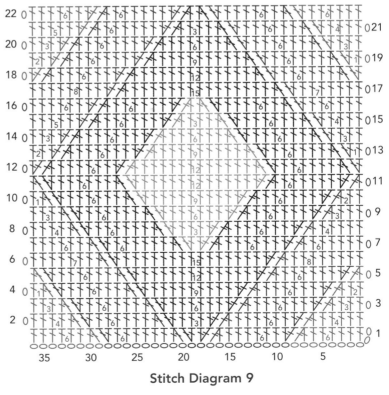

Stitch Diagram 9

ROW 17: Ch 1, dc in first 7 dc, *carry D under* 2 dc in next dc, change to D, dc2tog, dc in next 15 dc, dc2tog, change to B, 2 dc in next dc, dc in next 8 dc, change to A, turn—9 B, 17 D, 10 B.

ROW 18: Ch 1, *carry B under* 2 dc in next dc, change to B, dc2tog, dc in next 6 dc, *carry D under* 2 dc in next dc, change to D, dc2tog, dc in next 12 dc, dc2tog, change to B, 2 dc in next dc, dc in next 6 dc, dc2tog, change to A, 2 dc in last dc, turn— 2 A, 9 B, 14 D, 9 B, 2 A.

ROWS 19–21: Ch 1, dc in each dc to last A-color dc, *carry B under* 2 dc in next dc, change to B, dc2tog, dc in next 6 dc, *carry D under* 2 dc in next dc, change to D, dc2tog, dc in each dc to last 3 D-color dc, dc2tog, change to B, 2 dc in next dc, dc in next 6 dc, dc2tog, change to A, 2 dc in next dc, dc across, turn.

ROW 22: Ch 1, dc in first 6 dc, *carry B under* 2 dc in next dc, change to B, dc2tog, dc in next 6 dc, *carry D under* 2 dc in next dc, change to D, 2 dc2tog, change to B, 2 dc in next dc, dc in next 6 dc, dc2tog, change to A, 2 dc in next dc, dc across. Finish off and weave in ends—8 A, 9 B, 2 D, 9 B, 8 A.

SQUARE

10

Waves

Double Crochet Half-Color Stitch

In this square, you'll learn some of the stitches that are unique to the reversible intarsia technique when working with double crochets. By working the top half of the stitch in one color and the bottom half in another color, you can create greater detail in your images. This square alternates rows of double crochet reversible color changes with rows of half-color stitches to create an upright wave pattern.

Notes

- See Pattern Notes in Square 3, and Pattern Notes for All Squares on page 16.

- Letters in parenthesis following each ½-color dc stitch indicate which colors should be on the top/bottom of the ½-color stitch.

- Always carry new color under last stitch before color change *or* first ½-color dc using new color (indicated in this square with special instructions in italics).

- Refer to Special Stitches: Double Crochet Reversible Color Change (change to); Half-Color Double Crochet (½-color dc) and Half-Color Double Crochet Color Change.

- Refer to Stitch Diagram 10 on page 41 for assistance.

Pattern

With D, ch 10, attach C, ch 10, attach B, ch 10, attach A, ch 8—38 ch.

ROW 1: Dc in third ch from hook and next 5 ch, ½-color dc (A/B) in next ch, change to B, dc in next 9 ch, ½-color dc (B/C), change to C, dc in next 9 ch, ½-color dc (C/D), change to D, dc across, turn—7 A, 10 B, 10 C, 9 D (36 dc).

ROW 2: Ch 1, dc in each dc to last D-color dc, change to C, dc in next 10 dc, change to B, dc, dc in next 10 dc, change to A, dc, dc across, turn.

ROW 3: Ch 1, dc in each A-color dc *carrying B under final dc*, ½-color dc (A/B), change to B, dc in next 9 dc, *carrying C under final dc*, ½-color dc (B/C), change to C, dc in next 9 dc, *carrying B under final dc*, ½-color dc (C/D), change to D, dc across, turn.

ROW 4: Rep Row 2.

ROW 5: Ch 1, dc in first 10 dc, change to B, dc in next 10 dc, change to C, dc in next 10 dc, change to D, dc across, turn—10 A, 10 B, 10 C, 6 D.

ROW 6: Ch 1, dc in each D-color dc, *carrying C under final dc*, ½-color dc (D/C), change to C, dc in next 9 dc, *carrying B under final dc*, ½-color dc (C/B), change to B, dc in next 9 dc, *carrying A under final dc*, ½-color dc (B/A), change to A, dc across, turn.

ROW 7: Ch 1, dc in each dc to last A-color dc, change to B, dc in next 10 dc, change to C, dc in next 10 dc, change to D, dc across, turn.

ROWS 8–10: Alternate Rows 6 and 7.

ROW 11: Ch 1, dc in first 5 dc, change to B, dc in next 10 dc, change to C, dc in next 10 dc, change to D, dc across, turn—5 A, 10 B, 10 C, 11 D.

ROW 12: Ch 1, dc in first 11 dc, change to C, dc in next 10 dc, change to B, dc in next 10 dc, change to A, dc across, turn—11 D, 10 C, 10 B, 5 A.

ROWS 13–17: Alternate Rows 3 and 2.

ROW 18: Ch 1, dc in first 6 dc, change to C, dc in next 10 dc, change to B, dc in next 10 dc, change to A, dc across, turn—6 D, 10 C, 10 B, 10 A.

ROWS 19–22: Rep Rows 5–8. Fasten off all colors and weave in ends.

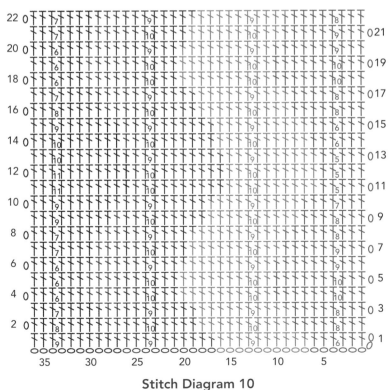

Stitch Diagram 10

Arrows

Reverse Half-Color Double Crochet

In the previous square, you learned how to work double crochet stitches with the top half in one color and the bottom half in another. Now, you'll learn to work the same stitch in the opposite direction. This can be a bit tricky because you have to work the bottom half of the stitch under the strand of yarn that was carried over for the top color. But don't worry, this square will give you the chance to perfect the technique.

Notes

- See Pattern Notes for All Squares on page 16.

- Letters in parenthesis following each ½-color dc stitch indicate which colors should be on the top/bottom of the ½-color stitch.

- Always carry new color under last stitch of previous color to bring it up into the stitch, except before a rev½-color dc, when the yarn is coming toward your hook (rather than being under your hook).

- Before a rev½-color dc, you will work a regular color change; do not flip yarn up after change as with other reversible stitches.

- The yarn strand of the top color is hidden between the top and bottom halves of the rev½-color dc.

- Refer to Special Stitches: Reversible Color Change (change to) and Reverse Half-Color Double Crochet (rev½-color dc).

- Refer to Stitch Diagram 11 on page 43 for assistance.

Pattern

With C, ch 14, attach D, ch 9, attach B, ch 9, attach A, ch 6—38 ch.

ROW 1: Dc in third ch from hook and next 3 ch, change to B, dc in next 9 dc, change to D, dc in next 9 dc, change to C, dc across, turn—4 A, 9 B, 9 D, 14 C (36 dc).

ROW 2: Ch 1, dc in each dc to last 2 C-color dc, change to D, rev½-color dc (D/C), dc in next 8 dc, change to B, rev½-color dc (B/D), dc in next 8 dc, change to A, rev½-color dc (A/B), dc across, turn—12 C, 9 D, 9 B, 6 A.

ROW 3: Ch 1, dc in each A-color dc, change to B, dc in next 9 dc, change to D, dc in next 9 dc, change to C, dc across, turn—6 A, 9 B, 9 D, 12 C.

ROWS 4–10: Alternate Rows 2 and 3, ending with Row 2—st count will vary each row.

ROW 11: Ch 1, dc in first 14 dc, change to B, dc in next 9 dc, change to D, dc in next 9 dc, change to C, dc across, turn—14 A, 9 B, 9 D, 4 C.

ROW 12: Ch 1, dc in each C-color dc, change to D, dc in next 9 dc, change to B, dc in next 9 dc, change to A, dc across, turn—4 C, 9 D, 9 B, 14 A.

ROW 13: Ch 1, dc in each dc to last 2 A-color dc, change to B, rev½-color dc (B/A), dc in next 8 dc, change to D, rev½-color dc (D/B), dc in next 8 dc, change to C, rev½-color dc (C/D), dc across, turn—12 A, 9 B, 9 D, 6 C.

ROWS 14–22: Alternate Rows 12 and 13, ending with Row 12—st count will vary each row. Fasten off all colors and weave in ends.

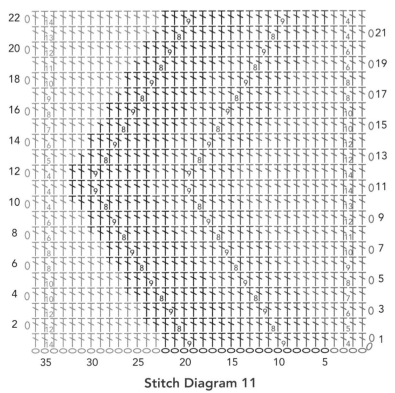

Stitch Diagram 11

SQUARE

12

Bulls-eye

Quilt Square

Now is the time to mix it up, combining increases and decreases with half-color stitches to create double crochet circles-within-circles. After completing this final "learning square," you'll have the tools you need to branch out and create all kinds of exciting reversible intarsia designs!

Notes

- See Pattern Notes for All Squares on page 16.

- Letters in parenthesis following each ½-color dc stitch indicate which colors should be on the top/bottom of the ½-color stitch.

- Always carry new color under last stitch of previous color to bring it up into the stitch. Italics are used to indicate all other times it is necessary to carry yarn before a color change.

- See Special Stitches: Reversible Color Change (change to), Reverse Half-Color Double Crochet (rev½-color dc), Half-Color Double Crochet (½-color dc).

- Refer to Stitch Diagram 12 on page 45 for assistance.

Pattern

With A, ch 38.

ROW 1: Dc in third ch from hook and each ch across, turn—36 dc.

ROW 2: Ch 1, dc in first 12 dc, change to D, do not flip yarn, ½-color dc (D/A) in next 3 dc, *carry A under* dc in next 6 dc, ½-color dc (D/A) in next 3 dc, change to A, dc across, turn—12 A, 12 D, 12 A.

ROW 3: Ch 1, dc in first 9 dc, dc2tog, change to D, 2 dc in next dc, dc in next 12 dc, 2 dc in next dc, change to *new ball* A, dc2tog, dc across, turn—10 A, 16 D, 10 A.

ROW 4: Ch 1, dc in first 7 dc, dc2tog, change to D, 2 dc in next dc, dc in next 16 dc, *carry A under* 2 dc in next dc, change to A, dc2tog, dc across, turn—8 A, 20 D, 8 A.

ROW 5: Ch 1, dc in first 5 dc, dc2tog, change to D, 2 dc in next dc, dc in next 19 dc, *carry A under* 2 dc in next dc, change to A, dc2tog, dc across, turn—6 A, 23 D, 7 A.

ROW 6: Ch 1, dc in first 4 dc, dc2tog, change to D, 2 dc in next dc, dc in next 7 dc, change to C, ½-color dc (C/D) in next 2 dc, *carry D under* dc in next 4 dc, ½-color dc (C/D) in next 2 dc, change to D, dc in next 7 dc, *carry A under previous dc* and 2 dc in next dc, change to A, dc2tog, dc across, turn—5 A, 9 D, 8 C, 9 D, 5 A.

ROW 7: Ch 1, dc in first 3 dc, dc2tog, change to D, 2 dc in next dc, dc in next 5 dc, dc2tog, change to C, 2 dc in next dc, dc in next 8 dc, 2 dc in next dc, change to D, dc2tog, dc in next 5 dc, 2 dc in next dc, change to A, *carry A under* dc2tog, dc across, turn—4 A, 8 D, 12 C, 8 D, 4 A.

ROW 8: Ch 1, dc in first 2 dc, dc2tog, change to D, 2 dc in next dc, dc in next 4 dc, dc2tog, change to C, 2 dc in next dc, dc in next 12 dc, *carry D under previous dc* and 2 dc in next dc, change to D, dc2tog, dc in next 4 dc, *carry A under* 2 dc in next dc, change to A, dc2tog, dc across, turn—3 A, 7 D, 16 C, 7 D, 3 A.

ROW 9: Ch 1, dc in first 3 dc *carrying D under final dc,* change to D, dc in next 5 dc, *carry C under second st of next* dc2tog, change to C, 2 dc in next dc, dc in next 14 dc, *carry D under* 2 dc in next dc, change to D, dc2tog, dc in next 5 dc *carrying A under final dc,* change to A, dc across, turn—3 A, 6 D, 18 C, 6 D, 3 A.

ROW 10: Ch 1, dc in first 2 dc, change to D, dc in next 5 dc, *carry C under second st of next* dc2tog, change to C, 2 dc in next dc, dc in next 6 dc, change to B, ½-color dc (B/C), *carry C under* dc in next 2 dc, ½-color dc (B/C), change to C, dc in next 6 dc, *carry D under* 2 dc in next dc, change to D, dc2tog, dc in next 5 dc, change to A, dc across, turn—2 A, 6 D, 8 C, 4 B, 8 C, 6 D, 2 A.

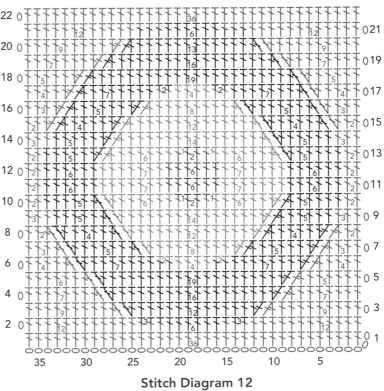

Stitch Diagram 12

ROWS 11 AND 12: Ch 1, dc in first 2 dc, change to D, dc in next 6 dc, change to C, dc in next 7 dc, change to B, dc in next 6 dc, change to C, dc in next 7 dc, change to D, dc in next 6 dc, change to A, dc across, turn—2 A, 6 D, 7 C, 6 B, 7 C, 6 D, 2 A.

ROW 13: Ch 1, dc in first 2 dc, change to D, dc in next 5 dc, *carry C under* 2 dc in next dc, change to C, dc2tog, dc in next 6 dc, ½-color dc (C/B), change to B, dc in next 2 dc, change to C, rev ½-color dc (C/B), dc in next 6 dc, *carry D under second st of next* dc2tog, change to D, 2 dc in next dc, dc in next 5 dc, change to A, dc across, turn. *Cut off B and first C*—2 A, 7 D, 8 C, 2 B, 8 C, 7 D, 2 A.

ROW 14: Ch 1, dc in first 3 dc, change to D, dc in next 5 dc, *carry C under* 2 dc in next dc, change to C, dc2tog, dc in next 14 dc, dc2tog, change to D, 2 dc in next dc, dc in next 5 dc, change to A, dc across, turn—3 A, 7 D, 16 C, 7 D, 3 A.

ROW 15: Ch 1, dc in first 2 dc, *carry D under* 2 dc in next dc, change to D, dc2tog, dc in next 4 dc, *carry C under previous dc and* 2 dc in next dc, change to C, dc2tog, dc in next 12 dc, dc2tog, change to D, 2 dc in next dc, dc in next 4 dc, *carry A under second st of* dc2tog, change to A, 2 dc in next dc, dc across, turn—4 A, 7 D, 14 C, 7 D, 4 A.

ROW 16: Ch 1, dc in first 3 dc, *carry D under* 2 dc in next dc, change to D, dc2tog, dc in next 5 dc, *carry C under previous dc and* 2 dc in next dc, change to C, dc2tog, dc in next 8 dc, dc2tog, change to D, 2 dc in next dc, dc in

next 5 dc, *carry A under second st of next* dc2tog, change to A, 2 dc in next dc, dc across, turn—5 A, 8 D, 10 C, 8 D, 5 A.

ROW 17: Ch 1, dc in first 4 dc, 2 dc in next dc, change to D, dc2tog, dc in next 7 dc *carrying C under final* 2 dc, ½-color dc (D/C) in next 2 dc, change to C, dc in next 4 dc, change to D, rev ½-color dc (D/C) in next 2 dc, dc in next 7 dc, dc2tog, change to A, 2 dc in next dc, dc across, turn—6 A, 10 D, 4 C, 10 D, 6 A.

ROW 18: Ch 1, dc in first 5 dc, *carry D under previous dc and* 2 dc in next dc, change to D, dc2tog, dc in next 19 dc, dc2tog, change to A, 2 dc in next dc, dc across, turn—7 A, 21 D, 8 A.

ROW 19: Ch 1, dc in first 7 dc, *carry D under previous dc and* 2 dc in next dc, change to D, dc2tog, dc in next 16 dc, dc2tog, change to A, 2 dc in next dc, dc across, turn—9 A, 18 D, 9 A.

ROW 20: Ch 1, dc in next 9 dc, *carry D under* previous dc and 2 dc in next dc, change to D, dc2tog, dc in next 12 dc, dc2tog, change to A, 2 dc in next dc, dc across, turn—11 A, 14 D, 11 A.

ROW 21: Ch 1, dc in first 12 dc, *carrying D under final* 2 dc, ½-color dc (A/D) in next 3 dc, change to D, dc in next 6 dc, change to A carrying A across top of 4 sts, rev ½-color dc (C/D) in next 3 sts, dc across, turn—15 A, 6 D, 15 A.

ROW 22: Ch 1, dc in each dc across. Fasten off all colors and weave in ends.

PART 4:
Quilting with a Hook

Now comes the really fun part, combining all those stitches you learned in the previous sections to create shapes! Much like quilting with fabric, most quilt-inspired crochet and knit patterns involve stitching together small shapes of different colors to create a design. All of that stitching can make this process seem daunting, so why not try working the same patterns in rows of the most basic half double and double crochet stitches? Although juggling multiple colors of yarn at the same time may seem equally daunting, once your fingers have learned how to handle the yarn, anything is possible.

Double Friendship Star

Notes

- See Pattern Notes for All Squares on page 16.

- Always carry the strand of the new color under both stitches of an increase (2 hdc in the same stitch) worked just before a late color change followed by a decrease (hdc-sc-tog).

- Carry the strand of the new color under the second stitch of a decrease (hdc-sc-tog) followed by an increase.

- As indicated in the pattern, on some angles, color change will be on first yo of the first stitch (see Late Color Change in Special Stitches, page 11).

- Refer to Stitch Diagram 13 on page 49 for assistance.

Pattern

With A, ch 37.

ROW 1: Ch 1, hdc in third ch from hook and next 11 ch, change to D, hdc in next ch, late change to A, hdc in next 10 ch, change to B, hdc in next ch, change to A, hdc across, turn—12 A, 2 D, 9 A, 1 B, 12 A (36 hdc).

ROW 2: Ch 1, hdc in first 12 hdc, change to B, 2 hdc in next hdc, late change to A, hdc-sc-tog, hdc in next 7 hdc, change to D, hdc in next 2 hdc, change to A, hdc across, turn—12 A, 3 B, 7 A, 2 D, 12 A.

ROW 3: Ch 1, hdc in first 12 hdc, change to D, hdc in next hdc, 2 hdc in next hdc, late change to A, hdc-sc-tog, hdc in next 3 hdc, hdc-sc-tog, change to B, 2 hdc in next hdc, hdc in next 2 hdc, change to A, hdc across, turn—12 A, 4 D, 4 A, 4 B, 12 A.

ROW 4: Ch 1, hdc in first 12 hdc, change to B, hdc in next 3 hdc, 2 hdc in next hdc, late change to A, hdc-sc-tog, hdc in next 2 hdc, change to D, hdc in next 4 hdc, change to A, hdc across, turn—12 A, 6 B, 2 A, 4 D, 12 A.

ROW 5: Ch 1, hdc in first 12 hdc, change to D, hdc in next 3 hdc, 2 hdc in next hdc, late change to A, hdc-sc-tog, change to B, hdc in next 6 hdc, change to A, hdc across, turn—12 A, 6 D, 6 B, 12 A.

ROW 6: Ch 1, hdc in first 12 hdc, change to B, hdc in next 4 hdc, hdc-sc-tog, change to D, 2 hdc in next hdc, hdc in next 5 hdc, change to A, hdc across, turn—12 A, 5 B, 7 D, 12 A.

ROW 7: Ch 1, hdc in first 12 hdc, change to D, hdc in next 7 hdc, late change to B, hdc in next 5 hdc, change to A, hdc across, turn—12 A, 8 D, 4 B, 12 A.

ROW 8: Ch 1, hdc in first 12 hdc, change to B, hdc in next 2 hdc, hdc-sc-tog, change to D, 2 hdc in next hdc, hdc in next 7 hdc, change to A, hdc across, turn—12 A, 3 B, 9 D, 12 A.

ROW 9: Ch 1, hdc in first 12 hdc, change to D, hdc in next 8 hdc, 2 hdc in next hdc, late change to B, hdc-sc-tog, hdc in next hdc, change to A, hdc across, turn—12A, 11 D, 1 B, 12 A.

ROW 10: Ch 1, hdc in first 12 hdc, change to B, hdc in next hdc, change to D, hdc in next 11 hdc, change to A, hdc across, turn—12 A, 1 B, 11 D, 12 A.

ROW 11: Ch 1, hdc in first hdc, late change to B, hdc-sc-tog in last hdc used and next hdc, hdc in next 8 hdc, hdc-sc-tog, change to D, hdc in same st as last st made, change to C, hdc in next 12 hdc, change to D, hdc in next 10 hdc, hdc-sc-tog, change to A, hdc in same st as last st made, turn—2 A, 9 B, 1 D, 12 C, 11 D, 1 A.

ROW 12: Ch 1, 2 hdc in first hdc, late change to D, hdc-sc-tog, hdc in next 9 hdc, change to C, hdc in next 12 hdc, change to D, 2 hdc in next hdc, late change to B, hdc-sc-tog, hdc in next 5 hdc, hdc-sc-tog, change to A, 2 hdc in next hdc, hdc in last hdc, turn—3 A, 9 D, 12 C, 3 D, 6 B, 3 A.

ROW 13: Ch 1, hdc in first 2 hdc, 2 hdc in next hdc, late change to B, hdc-sc-tog, hdc in next 2 hdc, hdc-sc-tog, change to D, 2 hdc in next hdc, hdc in next 2 hdc, change to C, hdc in next 12 hdc, change to D, hdc in next 9 hdc, change to A, hdc across, turn—5 A, 3 B, 4 D, 12 C, 9 D, 3 A.

ROW 14: Ch 1, hdc in first 2 hdc, 2 hdc in next hdc, late change to D, hdc-sc-tog, hdc in next 7 hdc, change to C, hdc in next 12 hdc, change to D, hdc in next 4 hdc, late change to B, hdc in next 3 hdc, change to A, hdc across, turn—5 A, 7 D, 12 C, 5 D, 2 B, 5 A.

ROW 15: Ch 1, hdc in first 4 hdc, 2 hdc in next hdc, late change to B, hdc-sc-tog, change to D, hdc in next 5 hdc, change to C, hdc in next 12 hdc, change to D, hdc in next 5 hdc, hdc-sc-tog, change to A, 2 hdc in next hdc, hdc across, turn—7 A, 5 D, 12 C, 6 D, 6 A.

ROW 16: Ch 1, hdc in first 5 hdc, change to B, 2 hdc in next hdc, late change to D, hdc-sc-tog, hdc in next 4 hdc, change to C, hdc in

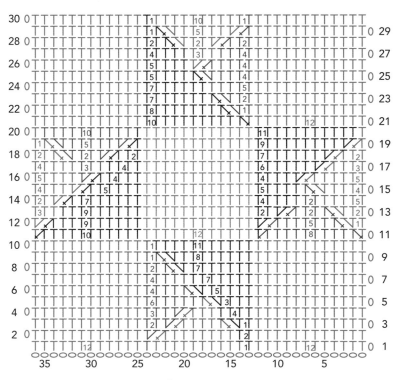

Stitch Diagram 13

next 12 hdc, change to D, hdc in next 4 hdc, 2 hdc in next hdc, late change to A, hdc-sc-tog, hdc across, turn—5 A, 3 B, 4 D, 12 C, 7 D, 5 A.

ROW 17: Ch 1, hdc in first 3 hdc, hdc-sc-tog, change to D, 2 hdc in next hdc, hdc in next 6 hdc, change to C, hdc in next 12 hdc, change to D, hdc in next 4 hdc, change to B, hdc in next 3 hdc, late change to A, hdc across, turn—4 A, 8 D, 12 C, 4 D, 4 B, 4 A.

ROW 18: Ch 1, hdc in first 2 hdc, hdc-sc-tog, change to B, 2 hdc in next hdc, hdc in next 2 hdc, 2 hdc in next hdc, late change to D, hdc-sc-tog, hdc in next 2 hdc, change to C, hdc in next 12 hdc, change to D, hdc in next 7 hdc, 2 hdc in next hdc, late change to A, hdc-sc-tog, hdc across, turn—3 A, 7 B, 2 D, 12 C, 10 D, 2 A.

ROW 19: Ch 1, hdc-sc-tog, change to D, 2 hdc in next hdc, hdc in next 9 hdc, change to C, hdc in next 12 hdc, change to D, hdc-sc-tog, change to B, 2 hdc in next hdc, hdc in next 5 hdc, 2 hdc in next hdc, late change to A, hdc-sc-tog, hdc in last hdc, turn—1 A, 11 D, 12 C, 1 D, 10 B, 1 A.

ROW 20: Ch 1, hdc in first hdc, change to B, hdc in next 10 hdc, late change to D, hdc in next hdc, change to C, hdc in next 12 hdc, change to D, hdc in next 11 hdc, late change to A, hdc in last hdc, turn—1 A, 11 B, 12 C, 12 A.

ROW 21: Ch 1, hdc in first 12 hdc, change to B, hdc in next hdc, late change to D, hdc-sc-tog in last hdc used and next hdc, hdc in next 10 hdc, change to A, hdc across, turn—12 A, 2 B, 10 D, 12 A.

ROW 22: Ch 1, hdc in first 12 hdc, change to D, hdc in next 8 hdc, hdc-sc-tog, change to B, 2 hdc in next hdc, hdc in next hdc, change to A, hdc across, turn—12 A, 9 B, 3 D, 12 A.

ROW 23: Ch 1, hdc in first 12 hdc, change to B, hdc in next 2 hdc, 2 hdc in next hdc, late change to D, hdc-sc-tog, hdc in next 7 hdc, change to A, hdc across, turn—12 A, 5 B, 7 D, 12 A.

ROW 24: Ch 1, hdc in first 12 hdc, change to D, hdc in next 7 hdc, change to B, hdc in next 5 hdc, change to A, hdc across, turn—12 A, 7 B, 5 D, 12 A.

ROW 25: Ch 1, hdc in first 12 hdc, change to B, hdc in next 4 hdc, 2 hdc in next hdc, late change to D, hdc-sc-tog, hdc in next 5 hdc, change to A, hdc across, turn—12 A, 7 B, 5 D, 12 A.

ROW 26: Ch 1, hdc in first 12 hdc, change to D, hdc in next 5 hdc, change to A, 2 hdc in next hdc, late change to B, hdc-sc-tog, hdc in next 4 hdc, change to A, hdc across, turn—12 A, 5 D, 3 A, 4 B, 12 A.

ROW 27: Ch 1, hdc in first 12 hdc, change to B, hdc in next 4 hdc, change to A, hdc in next 3 hdc, late change to D, hdc in next 5 hdc, change to A, hdc across, turn—12 A, 4 B, 4 A, 4 D, 12 A.

ROW 28: Ch 1, hdc in first 12 hdc, change to D, hdc in next 2 hdc, hdc-sc-tog, change to A, 2 hdc in next hdc, hdc in next 2 hdc, 2 hdc in next hdc, late change to B, hdc-sc-tog, hdc in next 2 hdc, change to A, hdc across, turn— 12 A, 3 D, 7 A, 2 B, 12 A.

ROW 29: Ch 1, hdc in first 12 hdc, change to B, hdc-sc-tog, change to A, 2 hdc in next hdc, hdc in next 5 hdc, 2 hdc in next hdc, late change to D, hdc-sc-tog, hdc in next hdc, change to A, hdc across, turn—12 A, 1 B, 10 A, 1 D, 12 A.

ROW 30: Ch 1, hdc in first 12 hdc, late change to D, hdc in next hdc, change to A, hdc in next 10 hdc, late change to B, hdc in next hdc, change to A, hdc across, turn—36 A. Fasten off all colors and weave in ends.

SQUARE

14

Card Trick

Notes

- See Pattern Notes for All Squares on page 16.

- Always carry the strand of the new color under both stitches of an increase (2 hdc in the same stitch) worked just before a late color change followed by a decrease (hdc-sc-tog).

- Carry the strand of the new color under the second stitch of a decrease (hdc-sc-tog) followed by an increase.

- As indicated in the pattern, on some angles, color change will be on the first yo of the first stitch (see Late Color Change in Special Stitches, page 11).

- Refer to Stitch Diagram 14 on page 52.

Pattern

With A, ch 37.

ROW 1: Hdc in second ch from hook and next 11 ch, change to B, 2 hdc in next ch, late change to A, hdc-sc-tog, hdc in next 6 ch, hdc-sc-tog, change to D, 2 hdc in next ch, late change to A, hdc each ch across, turn—12 A, 3 B, 7 A, 3 D, 11 A (36 hdc).

ROW 2: Ch 1, hdc in first 11 hdc, change to D, hdc in next 2 hdc, 2 hdc in next hdc, late change to A, hdc-sc-tog, hdc in next 5 hdc, change to B, hdc in next 2 hdc, 2 hdc in next hdc, late change to A, hdc-sc-tog, hdc across, turn—11 A, 5 D, 5 A, 5 B, 10 A.

ROW 3: Ch 1, hdc in first 10 hdc, change to B, hdc in next 4 hdc, 2 hdc in next hdc, late change to A, hdc-sc-tog, hdc in next 3 hdc, change to D, hdc in next 4 hdc, 2 hdc in next hdc, late change to A, hdc-sc-tog, hdc across, turn—10 A, 7 B, 3 A, 7 D, 9 A.

Chapter 2: Learning and "Quilt" Squares **51**

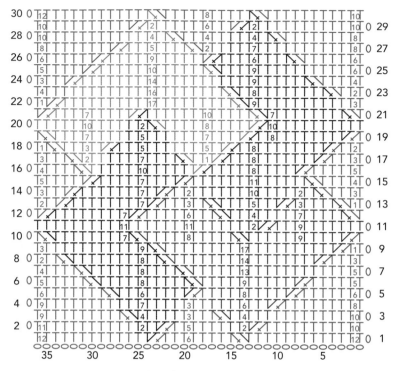

Stitch Diagram 14

ROW 4: Ch 1, hdc in first 9 hdc, change to D, hdc in next 7 hdc, late change to A, hdc in next 3 hdc, change to B, hdc in next 6 hdc, 2 hdc in next hdc, late change to A, hdc-sc-tog, hdc across, turn—9 A, 8 D, 2 A, 9 B, 8 A.

ROW 5: Ch 1, hdc in first 6 hdc, hdc-sc-tog, change to B, 2 hdc in next hdc, hdc in next 8 hdc, late change to A, hdc-sc-tog, change to D, 2 hdc in next hdc, hdc in next 6 hdc, 2 hdc in next hdc, late change to A, hdc-sc-tog, hdc across, turn—7 A, 11 B, 11 D, 7 A.

ROW 6: Ch 1, hdc in first 5 hdc, hdc-sc-tog, change to D, 2 hdc in next hdc, hdc in next 8 hdc, hdc-sc-tog, change to B, 2 hdc in next hdc, hdc in next 9 hdc, 2 hdc in next hdc, late change to A, hdc-sc-tog, hdc across, turn—6 A, 11 D, 14 B, 5 A.

ROW 7: Ch 1, hdc in first 5 hdc, change to B, hdc in next 13 hdc, 2 hdc in next hdc, late change to D, hdc-sc-tog, hdc in next 8 hdc, 2 hdc in next hdc, late change to A, hdc-sc-tog, hdc across, turn—5 A, 16 B, 11 D, 4 A.

ROW 8: Ch 1, hdc in first 2 hdc, hdc-sc-tog, change to D, 2 hdc in next hdc, hdc in next 8 hdc, hdc-sc-tog, change to B, 2 hdc in next hdc, hdc in next 14 hdc, 2 hdc in next hdc, late change to A, hdc-sc-tog, hdc across, turn—3 A, 11 D, 19 B, 3 A.

ROW 9: Ch 1, hdc in first hdc, hdc-sc-tog, change to B, 2 hdc in next hdc, hdc in next 17 hdc, 2 hdc in next hdc, late change to D, hdc-sc-tog, hdc in next 9 hdc, late change to A, hdc across, turn—2 A, 22 B, 10 D, 2 A.

ROW 10: Ch 1, hdc-sc-tog, change to D, 2 hdc in next hdc, hdc in next 7 hdc, hdc-sc-tog, change to B, 2 hdc in next hdc, hdc in next 8 hdc, hdc-sc-tog, change to E, 2 hdc in next hdc, late change to B, hdc in next 9 hdc, 2 hdc in next hdc, late change to A, hdc-sc-tog, turn—1 A, 10 D, 11 B, 3 E, 11 B.

ROW 11: Ch 1, late change to B, hdc in next 9 hdc, hdc-sc-tog, change to E, 2 hdc in next hdc, hdc in next 2 hdc, late change to B, hdc in next 11 hdc, change to D, hdc across, change to A, turn—10 B, 5 E, 10 B, 11 D.

ROW 12: Ch 1, 2 hdc in first hdc, late change to D, hdc-sc-tog, hdc in next 7 hdc, 2 hdc in next hdc, late change to B, hdc-sc-tog, hdc in next 6 hdc, hdc-sc-tog, change to E, 2 hdc in next hdc, hdc in next 4 hdc, late change to B, hdc in next 7 hdc, hdc-sc-tog, change to A, 2 hdc in next hdc, turn—3 A, 10 D, 7 B, 7 E, 7 B, 2 A.

ROW 13: Ch 1, hdc in first hdc, 2 hdc in next hdc, late change to B, hdc-sc-tog, hdc in next 3 hdc, hdc-sc-tog, change to E, 2 hdc in next hdc, hdc in next 5 hdc, 2 hdc in next hdc, late change to B, hdc-sc-tog, hdc in next 3 hdc, hdc-sc-tog, change to D, 2 hdc in next hdc, hdc in next 7 hdc, hdc-sc-tog, change to A, 2 hdc in next hdc, hdc across, turn—4 A, 4 B, 10 E, 4 B, 10 D, 4 A.

ROW 14: Ch 1, hdc in first 3 hdc, 2 hdc in next hdc, late change to D, hdc-sc-tog, hdc in next 7 hdc, 2 hdc in next hdc, late change to B, hdc-sc-tog, hdc in next 2 hdc, change to E, hdc in next 10 hdc, late change to B, hdc in next 2 hdc, hdc-sc-tog, change to A, 2 hdc in next hdc, hdc across, turn—6 A, 10 D, 2 B, 11 E, 2 B, 5 A.

ROW 15: Ch 1, hdc in first 4 hdc, 2 hdc in next hdc, late change to B, hdc-sc-tog, change to E, hdc in next 11 hdc, change to B, hdc-sc-tog, change to D, 2 hdc in next hdc, hdc in next 7 hdc, hdc-sc-tog, change to A, 2 hdc in next hdc, hdc across, turn—7 A, 11 E, 1 B, 10 D, 7 A.

ROW 16: Ch 1, hdc in first 4 hdc, hdc-sc-tog, change to C, 2 hdc in next hdc, late change to D, hdc in next 10 hdc, change to C, 2 hdc in next hdc, late change to E, hdc-sc-tog, hdc in next 8 hdc, 2 hdc in next hdc, late change to A, hdc-sc-tog, hdc across, turn—5 A, 3 C, 9 D, 3 C, 11 E, 5 A.

ROW 17: Ch 1, hdc in first 3 hdc, hdc-sc-tog, change to E, 2 hdc in next hdc, hdc in next 8 hdc, hdc-sc-tog, change to C, 2 hdc in next hdc, hdc in next hdc, 2 hdc in next hdc, late change to D, hdc-sc-tog, hdc in next 7 hdc, change to C, hdc in next 2 hdc, 2 hdc in next hdc, late change to A, hdc-sc-tog, hdc across, turn—4 A, 11 E, 6 C, 7 D, 5 C, 3 A.

ROW 18: Ch 1, hdc in first hdc, hdc-sc-tog, change to C, 2 hdc in next hdc, hdc in next 3 hdc, 2 hdc in next hdc, late change to D, hdc-sc-tog, hdc in next 5 hdc, change to C, hdc in next 5 hdc, 2 hdc in next hdc, late change to E, hdc-sc-tog, hdc in next 8 hdc, 2 hdc in next hdc, late change to A, hdc-sc-tog, hdc across, turn—2 A, 8 C, 5 D, 8 C, 11 E, 2 A.

ROW 19: Ch 1, hdc-sc-tog, change to E, 2 hdc in next hdc, hdc in next 8 hdc, hdc-sc-tog, change to C, 2 hdc in next hdc, hdc in next 7 hdc, late change to D, hdc in next 5 hdc, change to C, hdc in next 7 hdc, 2 hdc in next hdc, late change to A, hdc-sc-tog, turn—1 A, 11 E, 10 C, 4 D, 10 C.

ROW 20: Ch 1, late change to C, hdc in first 10 hdc, late change to D, hdc in next 2 hdc, hdc-sc-tog, change to C, 2 hdc in next hdc, hdc in next 8 hdc, 2 hdc in next hdc, change to E, hdc-sc-tog, hdc across, change to A, turn—11 C, 2 D, 12 C, 11 E.

ROW 21: Ch 1, 2 hdc in first hdc, late change to E, hdc-sc-tog, hdc in next 7 hdc, 2 hdc in next hdc, late change to C, hdc-sc-tog, hdc in next 10 hdc, late change to D, hdc-sc-tog, change to C, 2 hdc in next hdc, hdc in next 7 hdc, hdc-sc-tog, change to A, 2 hdc in last hdc, turn—3 A, 10 E, 21 C, 2 A.

ROW 22: Ch 1, hdc in first hdc, 2 hdc in next hdc, late change to C, hdc-sc-tog, hdc in next 17 hdc, hdc-sc-tog, change to E, 2 hdc in next hdc, hdc in next 9 hdc, change to A, hdc across, turn—4 A, 18 C, 11 E, 3 A.

ROW 23: Ch 1, hdc in first 2 hdc, 2 hdc in next hdc, late change to E, hdc-sc-tog, hdc in next 8 hdc, 2 hdc in next hdc, late change to C, hdc-sc-tog, hdc in next 16 hdc, change to A, hdc across, turn—5 A, 11 E, 16 C, 4 A.

ROW 24: Ch 1, hdc in first 3 hdc, 2 hdc in next hdc, late change to C, hdc-sc-tog, hdc in next 14 hdc, change to E, hdc in next 9 hdc, hdc-sc-tog, change to A, 2 hdc in next hdc, hdc across, turn—6 A, 14 C, 10 E, 6 A.

ROW 25: Ch 1, hdc in first 6 hdc, late change to E, hdc in next 9 hdc, 2 hdc in next hdc, late change to C, hdc-sc-tog, hdc in next 10 hdc, hdc-sc-tog, change to A, 2 hdc in next hdc, hdc across, turn—7 A, 11 E, 11 C, 7 A.

ROW 26: Ch 1, hdc in first 6 hdc, 2 hdc in next hdc, late change to C, hdc-sc-tog, hdc in next 9 hdc, change to A, 2 hdc in next hdc, late change to E, hdc-sc-tog, hdc in next 6 hdc, hdc-sc-tog, change to A, 2 hdc in next hdc, hdc across, turn—9 A, 9 C, 3 A, 7 E, 8 A.

ROW 27: Ch 1, hdc in first 8 hdc, late change to E, hdc in next 7 hdc, change to A, hdc in next 2 hdc, 2 hdc in next hdc, late change to C, hdc-sc-tog, hdc in next 5 hdc, hdc-sc-tog, change to A, 2 hdc in next hdc, hdc across, turn—9 A, 6 E, 5 A, 6 C, 10 A.

ROW 28: Ch 1, hdc in first 10 hdc, late change to C, *hdc in next 4 hdc, hdc-sc-tog, change to A, 2 hdc in next hdc*, hdc in next 4 hdc, late change to E, rep from * to *, hdc across, turn—11 A, 4 C, 7 A, 4 E, 10 A.

ROW 29: Ch 1, hdc in first 10 hdc, late change to E, *hdc in next 2 hdc, hdc-sc-tog, change to A, 2 hdc in next hdc*, hdc in next 6 hdc, late change to C, rep from * to *, hdc across, turn—11 A, 2 E, 9 A, 2 C, 12 A.

ROW 30: Ch 1, hdc in first 12 hdc, late change to C, hdc-sc-tog, change to A, 2 hdc in next hdc, hdc in next 7 hdc, 2 hdc in next hdc, late change to E, hdc-sc-tog, change to A, hdc across, turn—36 A. Fasten off all colors and weave in ends.

Eight-Pointed Star

Notes

- See Pattern Notes for All Squares on page 16.

- Letters in parenthesis following each ½-color dc stitch indicate which colors should be on the top/bottom of the ½-color stitch.

- Always carry new color under last stitch of previous color to bring it up into the stitch, except before a rev½-color dc, when the yarn is coming toward your hook (rather than being under your hook).

- Refer to Stitch Diagram 15 on page 55 for assistance.

Pattern

With A, ch 38.

ROW 1: Dc in third ch from hook and next 9 ch, change to C, dc in next ch, ½-color dc (C/A) in next ch, change to A, dc in next 12 ch, change to D, ½-color dc (D/A) in next ch, dc in next ch, change to A, dc across, turn—10 A, 2 C, 12 A, 2 D, 10 A (36 dc).

ROW 2: Ch 1, dc in first 10 dc, change to D, dc in next dc, 2 dc in next dc, change to A, dc2tog, dc in next 8 dc, dc2tog, change to C, 2 dc in next dc, dc in next dc, change to A, dc across, turn—10 A, 3 D, 10 A, 3 C, 10 A.

ROW 3: Ch 1, dc in first 10 dc, change to C, dc in next 2 dc, 2 dc in next dc, change to A, dc2tog, dc in next 5 dc, dc2tog, change to D, 2 dc in next dc, dc in next 3 dc, change to A, dc across, turn—10 A, 4 C, 7 A, 5 D, 10 A.

ROW 4: Ch 1, dc in first 10 dc, change to D, dc in next 4 dc, 2 dc in next dc, change to A, dc2tog, dc in next 2 dc, dc2tog, change to C, 2 dc in next dc, dc in next 4 dc, change to A, dc across, turn—10 A, 6 D, 4 A, 6 C, 10 A.

ROW 5: Ch 1, dc first 10 dc, change to C, dc in next 5 dc, 2 dc in next dc, change to A, dc-3tog, change to D, 2 dc in next dc, dc in next 6 dc, change to A, dc across, turn—10 A, 7 C, 1 A, 8 D, 10 A.

ROW 6: Ch 1, dc in first 10 dc, change to D, dc in next 8 dc, change to C, dc in next 8 dc, change to A, dc across, turn—10 A, 8 D, 8 C, 10 A.

ROW 7: Ch 1, ½-color dc (A/D) in first dc, change to D, dc in next 8 dc, 2 dc in next dc, change to C, dc2tog, dc in next 6 dc, change to D, dc in next 6 dc, dc2tog, change to C, 2 dc in next dc, dc in next 8 dc, change to A, ½-color dc (A/C) in next dc, turn—1 A, 10 D, 7 C, 7 D, 10 C, 1 A.

ROW 8: Ch 1, 2 dc in first dc, change to C, dc2tog, dc in next 7 dc, 2 dc in next dc, change to D, dc2tog, dc in next 5 dc, change to C, dc in next 4 dc, dc2tog, change to D, 2 dc in next dc, dc in next 7 dc, dc2tog, change to A, 2 dc in next dc, dc in last dc, turn—2 C, 10 C, 6 D, 5 C, 10 D, 3 A.

ROW 9: Ch 1, dc in first 2 dc, 2 dc in next dc, change to D, dc2tog, dc in next 7 dc, 2 dc in next dc, change to C, dc2tog, dc in next 3 dc, change to D, dc in next 3 dc, dc2tog, change to C, 2 dc in next dc, dc in next 7 dc, dc2tog, change to A, 2 dc in next dc, dc in next 2 dc, turn—4 A, 10 D, 4 C, 4 D, 10 C, 4 A.

ROW 10: Ch 1, dc in first 4 dc, 2 dc in next dc, change to C, dc2tog, dc in next 6 dc, 2 dc in next dc, change to D, dc2tog, dc in next 2 dc, change to C, dc in next dc, dc2tog, change to D, 2 dc in next dc, dc in next 7 dc, dc2tog, change to A, 2 dc in next dc, dc across, turn—6 A, 9 C, 3 D, 2 C, 10 D, 6 A.

ROW 11: Ch 1, dc in first 6 dc, 2 dc in next dc, change to D, dc2tog, dc in next 6 dc, 2 dc in next dc, change to C, dc2tog, change to D, dc2tog, change to C, 2 dc in next dc, dc in next 6 dc, dc2tog, change to A, 2 dc in next dc, dc across, turn—8 A, 9 D, 1 C, 1 D, 9 C, 8 A.

ROW 12: Ch 1, dc in first 6 dc, dc2tog, change to D, 2 dc in next dc, dc in next 6 dc, dc2tog, change to C, 2 dc in next dc, change to D, 2 dc in next dc, change to C, dc2tog, dc in next 6 dc, 2 dc in next dc, change to A, dc2tog, dc across, turn—7 A, 9 D, 2 C, 2 D, 9 C, 7 A.

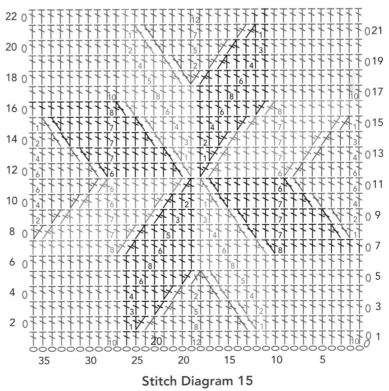

Stitch Diagram 15

ROW 13: Ch 1, dc in first 4 dc, dc2tog, change to C, 2 dc in next dc, dc in next 7 dc, dc2tog, change to D, 2 dc in next dc, dc in next dc, change to C, dc in next dc, 2 dc in next dc, change to D, dc2tog, dc in next 7 dc, 2 dc in next dc, change to A, dc2tog, dc across, turn—5 A, 10 C, 3 D, 3 C, 10 D, 5 A.

ROW 14: Ch 1, dc in first 2 dc, dc2tog, change to D, 2 dc in next dc, dc in next 7 dc, dc2tog, change to C, 2 dc in next dc, dc in next 3 dc, change to D, dc in next 2 dc, 2 dc in next dc, change to C, dc2tog, dc in next 7 dc, 2 dc in next dc, change to A, dc2tog, dc across, turn—3 A, 10 D, 5 C, 4 D, 10 C, 4 A.

ROW 15: Ch 1, dc in first dc, dc2tog, change to C, 2 dc in next dc, dc in next 7 dc, dc2tog, change to D, 2 dc in next dc, dc in next 4 dc, change to C, dc in next 4 dc, 2 dc in next dc, change to D, dc2tog, dc in next 7 dc, 2 dc in next dc, change to A, dc2tog, dc in last dc, turn—2 A, 10 C, 6 D, 6 C, 10 D, 2 A.

ROW 16: Change to D with ch 1, rev½-color dc (D/C) in next dc, dc in next 8 dc, dc2tog, change to C, 2 dc in next dc, dc in next 6 dc, change to D, dc in next 6 dc, 2 dc in next dc, change to C, dc2tog, dc in next 8 dc, ½-color dc (D/C) in next dc, change to A, turn—10 D, 8 C, 8 D, 10 C.

ROW 17: Rep Row 6.

ROW 18: Ch 1, dc first 10 dc, change to C, dc in next 5 dc, dc2tog, change to A, 3 dc in next dc, change to D, dc2tog, dc in next 6 dc, change to A, dc across, turn—10 A, 6 C, 3 A, 7 D, 10 A.

ROW 19: Ch 1, dc first 10 dc, change to D, dc in next 4 dc, dc2tog, change to A, 2 dc in next dc, dc in next 2 dc, 2 dc in next dc, change to C, dc2tog, dc in next 4 dc, change to A, dc across, turn—10 A, 5 D, 6 A, 5 C, 10 A.

ROW 20: Ch 1, dc first 10 dc, change to C, dc in next 2 dc, dc2tog, change to A, 2 dc in next dc, dc in next 5 dc, 2 dc in next dc, change to D, dc2tog, dc in next 3 dc, change to A, dc across, turn—10 A, 3 C, 9 A, 4 D, 10 A.

ROW 21: Ch 1, dc first 10 dc, change to D, dc in next dc, dc2tog, change to A, 2 dc in next dc, dc in next 8 dc, 2 dc in next dc, change to C, dc2tog, dc in next dc, change to A, dc across, turn—10 A, 2 D, 12 A, 2 C, 10 A.

ROW 22: Ch 1, dc first 10 dc, change to C, dc in next dc, change to A, rev½-color dc (A/C) in next dc, change to A, dc in next 12 dc, ½-color dc (A/D) in next dc, change to D, dc in next dc, change to A, dc across, turn—10 A, 1 C, 14 A, 1 D, 10 A. Fasten off all colors and weave in ends.

Snail's Trail

Notes

- See Pattern Notes for All Squares on page 16.

- Letters in parenthesis following each ½-color dc stitch indicate which colors should be on the top/bottom of the ½-color stitch.

- Always carry new color under last stitch of previous color to bring it up into the stitch, except before a rev½-color dc, when the yarn is coming toward your hook (rather than being under it).

- Refer to Stitch Diagram 16 on page 58.

Pattern

With B, ch 18, attach A, ch 20—38 ch.

ROW 1: Dc in third ch from hook and next 17 ch, 2 dc in next ch, change to B, dc2tog, dc across, turn—19 A, 17 B (36 dc).

ROW 2: Ch 1, dc in each dc to last 3 B-color dc, dc2tog, change to A, 2 dc in next dc, dc across, turn.

ROW 3: Ch 1, dc in each dc to last A-color dc, 2 dc in next dc, change to B, dc2tog, dc across, turn.

ROW 4: Rep Row 2—12 B, 24 A.

ROW 5: Ch 1, dc in first 11 dc, change to C, do not flip, ½-color dc (C/A) in next 5 dc, change to A, dc in next 7 dc, 2 dc in next dc, change to B, dc2tog, dc across, turn—11 A, 5 C, 9 A, 11 B.

ROW 6: Ch 1, dc in first 8 dc, dc2tog, change to A, 2 dc in next dc, dc in next 5 dc, change to C, rev½-color dc (C/A) in next 2 dc, dc in next 7 dc, 2 dc in next dc, change to A, dc2tog, dc across, turn—9 B, 7 A, 11 C, 9 A.

ROW 7: Ch 1, dc in first 6 dc, dc2tog, change to C, 2 dc in next dc, dc in next 11 dc, 2 dc in next dc, change to A, dc2tog, dc in next 3 dc, 2 dc in next dc, change to B, dc2tog, dc across, turn—7 A, 15 C, 6 A, 8 B.

ROW 8: Ch 1, dc in first 6 dc, dc2tog, change to A, 2 dc in next dc, dc in next 3 dc, dc2tog, change to C, 2 dc in next dc, dc in next 13 dc, 2 dc in next dc, change to A, dc2tog, dc across, turn—7 B, 6 A, 17 C, 6 A.

ROW 9: Ch 1, dc in first 3 dc, dc2tog, change to C, 2 dc in next dc, dc in next 5 dc, dc2tog, change to D, 2 dc in next dc, dc in next 2 dc,

2 dc in next dc, change to C, dc2tog, dc in next 3 dc, 2 dc in next dc, change to A, dc2tog, dc in next 4 dc, change to B, dc across, turn—4 A, 8 C, 6 D, 6 C, 5 A, 7 B.

ROW 10: Ch 1, dc in first 6 dc, 2 dc in next dc, change to A, dc2tog, dc in next 2 dc, 2 dc in next dc, change to C, dc2tog, dc in next dc, dc2tog, change to D, 2 dc in next dc, dc in next 5 dc, 2 dc in next dc, change to C, dc-2tog, dc in next 5 dc, 2 dc in next dc, change to A, dc2tog, dc across, turn—8 B, 5 A, 3 C, 9 D, 8 C, 3 A.

ROW 11: Ch 1, dc2tog, change to C, 2 dc in next dc, dc in next 5 dc, dc2tog, change to D, 2 dc in next dc, dc in next 2 dc, dc2tog, change to B, 2 dc in next 2 dc, change to D, dc3tog, change to C, 2 dc in next dc, dc2tog, change to A, 2 dc in next dc, dc in next 2 dc, dc2tog, change to B, 2 dc in next dc, dc across, change to D, turn—1 A, 8 C, 5 D, 4 B, 1 D, 3 C, 5 A, 9 B.

ROW 12: Ch 1, 2 dc in first dc, change to B, dc2tog, dc in first 5 dc, 2 dc in next dc, change to A, dc2tog, dc in next 2 dc, 2 dc in next dc, change to C, 2 dc2tog, change to A, 3 dc in next dc, change to B, dc2tog, 2 dc in next dc, change to D, dc2tog, dc in next 2 dc, 2 dc in next dc, change to C, dc2tog, dc across, turn—2 D, 8 B, 5 A, 2 C, 3 A, 3 B, 5 D, 8 C.

ROW 13: Ch 1, dc in first 6 dc, dc2tog, change to D, 2 dc in next dc, dc in next 2 dc, dc2tog, change to B, 2 dc in next dc, dc in next dc, 2 dc in next dc, change to A, dc2tog, dc in next 5 dc, dc2tog, change to B, 2 dc in next dc, dc in next 5 dc, dc2tog, change to D, 2 dc in next dc, dc across, turn—7 C, 5 D, 5 B, 7 A, 8 B, 4 D.

ROW 14: Ch 1, dc in first 3 dc, 2 dc in next dc, change to B, dc2tog, dc in next 5 dc, 2 dc in next dc, change to A, dc2tog, dc in next 2 dc, dc2tog, change to B, 2 dc in next dc, dc in next 3 dc, dc2tog, change to D, 2 dc in next dc, dc in next 4 dc, change to C, dc across, turn—5 D, 8 B, 4 A, 6 B, 6 D, 7 C.

ROW 15: Ch 1, dc in first 6 dc, 2 dc in next dc, change to D, dc2tog, dc in next 3 dc, 2 dc in next dc, change to B, dc2tog, dc in next 13 dc, dc2tog, change to D, 2 dc in next dc, dc across, turn—8 C, 6 D, 15 B, 7 D.

ROW 16: Ch 1, dc in first 6 dc, 2 dc in next dc, change to B, dc2tog, dc in next 11 dc, dc2tog, change to D, 2 dc in next dc, dc in next 3 dc, dc2tog, change to C, 2 dc in next dc, dc across, turn—8 D, 13 B, 6 D, 9 C.

ROW 17: Ch 1, dc in first 8 dc, 2 dc in next dc, change to D, dc2tog, dc in next 5 dc, ½-color dc (D/B) in next 2 dc, change to B, dc in next 7 dc, dc2tog, change to D, 2 dc in next dc, dc across, turn—10 C, 8 D, 8 B, 10 D.

ROW 18: Ch 1, dc in first 11 dc, ½-color dc (D/B) in next 5 dc, dc in next 7 dc, dc2tog, change to C, 2 dc in next dc, dc across, turn—24 D, 12 C.

ROWS 19–22: Alternate Rows 3 and 2. Fasten off all colors and weave in ends.

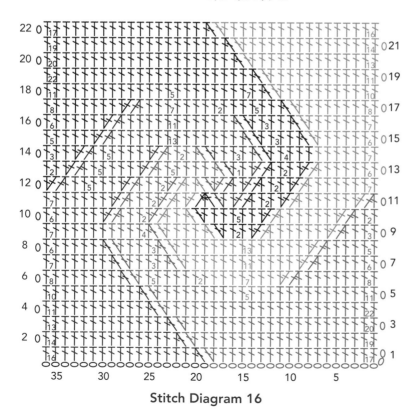

Stitch Diagram 16

CHAPTER 3
Picture Squares

PART 1:
Garden-Themed Squares

Now that you've learned the basics of working reversible stitches, you can create all sorts of images. Half double crochet is actually the ideal stitch for creating simple shapes and pictures. Single crochet stitches, for example, are less ideal for colorwork because the top half of each stitch is covered up by the stitches of the row above it. As a result, although single crochet fits better into a square grid pattern, you can only see the lower loop of each color stitch. Because of the extra yarnover in half double crochet, you can still see two loops of the color even after the next row is worked.

You will see how the use of late color changes and increases and decreases add to the possibilities for achieving the desired shapes, without the pixelated look you get from typical colorwork. On the other hand, because the half double crochet stitches are taller, they don't fit as neatly into a square grid, so you have to adjust your image to allow for the taller stitches. This section will explore the possibilities of shaping simple pictures with half double crochet stitches.

Yarn
Worsted weight (#4 Medium).

Shown Here: Berroco Comfort (50% super fine nylon, 50% super fine acrylic; 210 yd [193 m]/3.5 oz [100 g])

Color A: #9758 Crypto Crystaline (turquoise)

Color B: #9740 Seedling (light green)

Color C: #9742 Pimpernel (dark muted pink)

Color D: #9764 Lidfors (muted gold)

Color E: #9727 Spanish Brown

Color F: #9734 Liquorice (black)

(See Afghan Layouts for quantities for individual projects or estimate about 2 squares per 100 g ball.)

Important Note: Refer to page 16 for pattern notes, hook, gauge, and notions for all squares.

Garden Squares Color Key

Color A

Color B

Color C

Color D

Color E

Color F

Tulip

Yarn Colors

A (#9758 Crypto Crystaline),
B (#9740 Seedling), and C (#9742
Pimpernel); see previous page for
further information.

Notes

- See Pattern Notes for All Squares on page 16.

- Refer to Stitch Diagram 17 on page 62 for assistance.

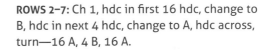

Pattern

With A, ch 16, fasten C, ch 4, fasten A,
ch 7—37 ch.

ROW 1: Hdc in second ch from hook and next
15 ch, change to B, hdc in next 4 ch, change
to A, hdc across, turn—16 A, 4 B, 16 A.

ROWS 2–7: Ch 1, hdc in first 16 hdc, change to
B, hdc in next 4 hdc, change to A, hdc across,
turn—16 A, 4 B, 16 A.

ROW 8: Ch 1, hdc in first 11 hdc, hdc-sc-tog,
change to C, 2 hdc in next hdc, hdc in next 7
hdc, 2 hdc in next hdc, late change to A, hdc-
sc-tog, hdc across, turn—12 A, 12 C, 12 A.

ROW 9: Ch 1, hdc in first 10 hdc, hdc-sc-tog,
change to C, 2 hdc in next hdc, hdc in next 10
hdc, 2 hdc in next hdc, late change to A, hdc-
sc-tog, hdc across, turn—11 A, 15 C, 10 A.

ROW 10: Ch 1, hdc in first 8 hdc, hdc-sc-tog,
change to C, 2 hdc in next hdc, hdc in next 13
hdc, 2 hdc in next hdc, late change to A, hdc-
sc-tog, hdc across, turn—9 A, 18 C, 9 A.

ROWS 11–14: Ch 1, hdc in each A-color hdc,
change to C, hdc in each B-color hdc, late
change to A, hdc across, turn.

ROWS 15–20: Ch 1, hdc in next 7 hdc, change
to C, hdc in next 22 hdc, change to A, hdc
across, turn—7 A, 22 C, 7 A.

ROW 21: Ch 1, hdc in next 7 hdc, change to C,
hdc in next 3 hdc, *hdc-sc-tog, change to A, 3
hdc in next hdc, late change to C, hdc-sc-tog*,
hdc in next 6 hdc, rep from * to *, hdc in next
3 hdc, change to A, hdc across, turn—7 A, 4 C,
4 A, 7 C, 4 A, 3 C, 7 A.

ROW 22: Ch 1, hdc in next 7 hdc, change to C, hdc in next 3 hdc, change to A, hdc in next 4 hdc, late change to C, hdc in next 7 hdc, change to A, hdc in next 4 hdc, late change to C, hdc in next 4 hdc, change to A, hdc across, turn—7 A, 3 C, 5 A, 6 C, 5 A, 3 C, 7 A.

ROW 23: Ch 1, hdc in next 7 hdc, change to C, hdc in next hdc, hdc-sc-tog, change to A, 2 hdc in next hdc, hdc in next 3 hdc, 2 hdc in next hdc, late change to C, hdc-sc-tog, hdc in next 2 hdc, hdc-sc-tog, change to A, 2 hdc in next hdc, hdc in next 3 hdc, 2 hdc in next hdc, change to C, hdc-sc-tog, hdc in next hdc, change to A, hdc across, turn—7 A, 2 C, 8 A, 3 C, 7 A, 2 C, 7 A.

ROW 24: Ch 1, hdc in next 7 hdc, late change to C, hdc-sc-tog, change to A, 2 hdc in next hdc, hdc in next 5 hdc, 2 hdc in next hdc, late change to C, hdc-sc-hdc-tog, change to A, 2 hdc in next hdc, hdc in next 6 hdc, 2 hdc in next hdc, late change to C, hdc-sc-tog, change to A, hdc across, turn—36 A.

ROWS 25–30: Ch 1, hdc in each hdc across, turn. Fasten off and weave in ends.

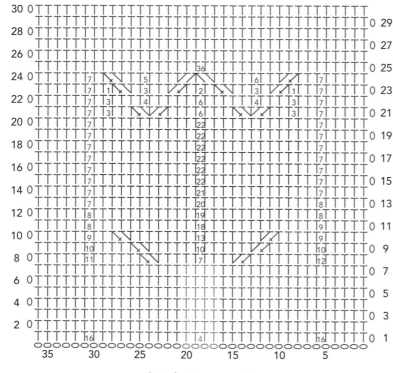

Stitch Diagram 17

Daisy

Yarn Colors
A (#9758 Crypto Crystaline), B (#9740 Seedling), D (#9764 Lidfors), and E (#9727 Spanish Brown); see page 60 for further information.

Notes
- See Pattern Notes for All Squares on page 16.
- Refer to Stitch Diagram 18 on page 64.

Pattern

With A, ch 16, join C, ch 4, join A, ch 17—37 ch.

ROW 1: Hdc in second ch from hook and next 15 ch, change to B, hdc in next 4 ch, change to A, hdc across, turn—16 A, 4 B, 16 A.

ROWS 2–4: Ch 1, hdc in first 16 hdc, change to B, hdc in next 4 hdc, change to A, hdc across, turn—16 A, 4 B, 16 A.

ROW 5: Ch 1, hdc in first 14 hdc, hdc-sc-tog, late change to B, hdc in next hdc, change to D, 2 hdc in each of next 2 hdc, late change to B, hdc in next hdc, change to A, hdc-sc-tog, hdc across, turn—16 A, 5 D, 15 A.

ROW 6: Ch 1, hdc in first 13 hdc, hdc-sc-tog, change to D, 2 hdc in next hdc, hdc in next 3 hdc, 2 hdc in next hdc, late change to A, hdc-sc-tog, hdc across, turn—14 A, 8 D, 14 A.

ROW 7: Ch 1, hdc in first 14 hdc, change to D, hdc in next 8 hdc, change to A, hdc across, turn—14 A, 8 D, 14 A.

ROW 8: Ch 1, hdc in first 5 hdc, hdc-sc-tog, change to D, 2 hdc in next hdc, hdc in next hdc, 2 hdc in next hdc, late change to A, hdc-sc-tog, hdc in next 2 hdc, change to D, hdc in next 8 hdc, change to A, hdc in next 2 hdc, hdc-sc-tog, change to D, 2 hdc in next hdc, hdc in next hdc, 2 hdc in next hdc, late change to A, hdc-sc-tog, hdc across, turn—6 A, 6 D, 2 A, 8 D, 3 A, 6 D, 5 A.

ROW 9: Ch 1, hdc in first 5 hdc, change to D, hdc in next 5 hdc, 2 hdc in next hdc, late change to A, hdc-sc-tog, hdc in next hdc, late change to D, hdc in next 8 hdc, change to A, hdc in next 2 hdc, change to D, hdc in next 6 hdc, late change to A, hdc across, turn—5 A, 8 D, 2 A, 7 D, 2 A, 7 D, 5 A.

ROW 10: Ch 1, hdc in first 5 hdc, change to D, hdc in next 7 hdc, late change to A, hdc in next 2 hdc, late change to D, hdc in next 7 hdc, change to A, hdc in next 2 hdc, change to D, hdc in next 8 hdc, change to A, hdc across, turn—5 A, 8 D, 2 A, 6 D, 2 A, 8 D, 5 A.

ROW 11: Ch 1, hdc in first 5 hdc, change to D, hdc in next 8 hdc, late change to A, hdc in next 2 hdc, late change to D, hdc in next 6 hdc, change to A, hdc in next 2 hdc, change to D, hdc in next 8 hdc, change to A, hdc across, turn—5 A, 9 D, 2 A, 5 D, 2 A, 8 D, 5 A.

ROW 12: Ch 1, hdc in first 5 hdc, late change to D, hdc in next 7 hdc, 2 hdc in next hdc, late change to A, hdc in next 2 hdc, change to D, hdc-sc-tog, hdc in next hdc, hdc-sc-tog, change

to A, hdc in next 2 hdc, change to D, 2 hdc in next hdc, hdc in next 8 hdc, change to A, hdc across, turn—6 A, 9 D, 1 A, 3 D, 2 A, 10 D, 5 A.

ROW 13: Ch 1, hdc in first 4 hdc, 2 hdc in next hdc, late change to D, hdc-sc-tog, hdc in next 7 hdc, hdc-sc-tog, change to E, 2 hdc in next hdc, hdc in next 2 hdc, 2 hdc in next hdc, late change to D, hdc-sc-tog, hdc in next 6 hdc, hdc-sc-tog, change to A, 2 hdc in next hdc, hdc across, turn—7 A, 8 D, 7 E, 7 D, 7 A.

ROW 14: Ch 1, hdc in first 6 hdc, 2 hdc in next hdc, late change to D, hdc-sc-tog, hdc in next 3 hdc, hdc-sc-tog, change to E, 2 hdc in next hdc, hdc in next 5 hdc, 2 hdc in next hdc, late change to D, hdc-sc-tog, hdc in next 4 hdc, hdc-sc-tog, change to A, 2 hdc in next hdc, hdc across, turn—9 A, 4 D, 10 E, 5 D, 8 A.

ROW 15: Ch 1, hdc in next 13 hdc, change to E, hdc in next 10 hdc, change to A, hdc across, turn—13 A, 10 E, 13 A.

ROW 16: Ch 1, hdc in next 13 hdc, late change to E, hdc in next 10 hdc, change to A, hdc across, turn—14 A, 9 E, 13 A.

ROW 17: Ch 1, hdc in first 5 hdc, hdc-sc-tog, change to D, 2 hdc in next hdc, hdc in next 4 hdc, 2 hdc in next hdc, late change to E, hdc-sc-tog, hdc in next 5 hdc, hdc-sc-tog, change to D, 2 hdc in next hdc, hdc in next 4 hdc, 2 hdc in next hdc, late change to A, hdc-sc-tog, hdc across, turn—6 A, 9 D, 6 E, 9 D, 6 A.

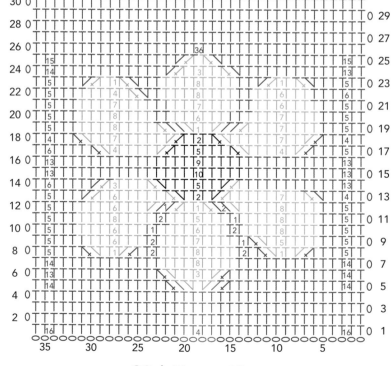

Stitch Diagram 18

ROW 18: Ch 1, hdc in first 4 hdc, hdc-sc-tog, change to D, 2 hdc in next hdc, hdc in next 7 hdc, 2 hdc in next hdc, change to E, hdc-sc-tog, hdc in next 2 hdc, hdc-sc-tog, change to D, 2 hdc in next hdc, hdc in next 7 hdc, 2 hdc in next hdc, change to A, hdc-sc-tog, hdc across, turn—5 A, 11 D, 4 E, 11 D, 5 A.

ROW 19: Ch 1, hdc in first 5 hdc, change to D, hdc in next 7 hdc, hdc-sc-tog, change to A, hdc in next 2 hdc, change to D, 2 hdc in next hdc, hdc in next hdc, 2 hdc in next hdc, late change to A, hdc in next 2 hdc, late change to D, hdc-sc-tog, hdc in next 8 hdc, change to A, hdc across, turn—5 A, 8 D, 2 A, 6 D, 2 A, 8 C, 5 A.

ROW 20: Ch 1, hdc in first 5 hdc, change to D, hdc in next 8 hdc, change to A, hdc in next 2 hdc, change to D, hdc in next 6 hdc, late change to A, hdc in next 2 hdc, late change to D, hdc in next 8 hdc, change to A, hdc across, turn—5 A, 8 D, 2 A, 7 D, 2 A, 7 D, 5 A.

ROW 21: Ch 1, hdc in first 5 hdc, late change to D, hdc in next 7 hdc, change to A, hdc in next 2 hdc, change to D, hdc in next 7 hdc, late change to A, hdc in next 2 hdc, late change to D, hdc in next 8 hdc, change to A, hdc across, turn—6 A, 6 D, 2 A, 8 D, 2 A, 7 D, 5 A.

ROW 22: Ch 1, hdc in first 5 hdc, late change to D, hdc in next 5 hdc, hdc-sc-tog, change to A, 2 hdc in next hdc, hdc in next hdc, change to D, hdc in next 8 hdc, change to A, hdc in next 2 hdc, late change to D, hdc in next 6 hdc, change to A, hdc across, turn—6 A, 5 D, 3 A, 8 D, 3 A, 5 D, 6 A.

ROW 23: Ch 1, hdc in next 5 hdc, 2 hdc in next hdc, late change to D, hdc-sc-tog, hdc in next hdc, hdc-sc-tog, change to A, 2 hdc in next hdc, hdc in next 2 hdc, change to D, hdc in next 8 hdc, change to A, hdc in next 2 hdc, 2 hdc in next hdc, late change to D, hdc-sc-tog, hdc in next hdc, hdc-sc-tog, change to A, 2 hdc in next hdc, hdc across, turn—8 A, 2 D, 4 A, 8 D, 5 A, 2 D, 7 A.

ROW 24: Ch 1, hdc in first 14 hdc, late change to D, hdc in next 8 hdc, change to A, hdc across, turn—15 A, 7 D, 14 A.

ROW 25: Ch 1, hdc in next 13 hdc, 2 hdc in next hdc, late change to D, hdc-sc-tog, hdc in next 3 hdc, hdc-sc-tog, change to A, 2 hdc in next hdc, hdc across, turn—16 A, 4 D, 16 A.

ROW 26: Ch 1, hdc in next 15 hdc, 2 hdc in next hdc, late change to D, 2 hdc-sc-tog, change to A, 2 hdc in next hdc, hdc across, turn—18 A, 1 D, 17 A.

ROWS 27–30: Ch 1, hdc in each hdc across, turn—36 A. Fasten off and weave in ends.

Alternative Daisy

To make a daisy only, without a stem, make the following changes: begin with A, ch 37, replace Rows 1–4 with Row 27, continue to work A where B is called for in Row 5.

Stem with Leaf

Yarn Colors

A (#9758 Crypto Crystaline) and B (#9740 Seedling); see page 60 for further information.

Notes

- See Pattern Notes for All Squares on page 16.
- Refer to Stitch Diagram 19 on page 67 for assistance.

Pattern

With A, ch 16, join C, ch 4, join A, ch 17—37 ch.

ROW 1: Hdc in second ch from hook and next 15 ch, change to B, hdc in next 4 ch, change to A, hdc in each ch across, turn—16 A, 4 B, 16 A.

ROWS 2–12: Ch 1, hdc in first 16 hdc, change to B, hdc in next 4 hdc, change to A, hdc in each ch across, turn—16 A, 4 B, 16 A.

ROW 13: Ch 1, hdc in first 16 hdc, change to B, hdc in next 3 hdc, 2 hdc in next hdc, late change to A, hdc-sc-tog, hdc across, turn—16 A, 6 B, 14 A.

ROW 14: Ch 1, hdc in first 12 hdc, hdc-sc-tog, change to B, 2 hdc in next hdc, hdc in next 5 hdc, change to A, hdc across, turn—13 A, 7 B, 16 A.

ROW 15: Ch 1, hdc in first 16 hdc, change to B, hdc in next 4 hdc, change to A, hdc in next hdc, late change to B, hdc in next 2 hdc, 2 hdc in next hdc, late change to A, hdc-sc-tog, hdc across, turn—16 A, 4 B, 2 A, 4 B, 10 A.

ROW 16: Ch 1, hdc in first 8 hdc, hdc-sc-tog, change to B, 2 hdc in next hdc, hdc in next 3 hdc, change to A, hdc in next 2 hdc, change to B, hdc in next 4 hdc, change to A, hdc across, turn—9 A, 5 B, 2 A, 4 B, 16 A.

ROW 17: Ch 1, hdc in first 16 hdc, change to B, hdc in next 4 hdc, change to A, hdc in next 2 hdc, late change to B, hdc in next 4 hdc, 2 hdc in next hdc, late change to A, hdc-sc-tog, hdc across, turn—16 A, 4 B, 3 A, 6 B, 7 A.

ROW 18: Ch 1, hdc in first 5 hdc, hdc-sc-tog, change to B, 2 hdc in next hdc, hdc in next 5 hdc, change to A, hdc in next 3 hdc, change to B, hdc in next 4 hdc, change to A, hdc across, turn—6 A, 7 B, 3 A, 4 B, 16 A.

ROW 19: Ch 1, hdc in first 16 hdc, change to B, hdc in next 4 hdc, change to A, hdc in next 3 hdc, late change to B, hdc in next 6 hdc, 2 hdc in next hdc, late change to A, hdc-sc-tog, hdc across, turn—16 A, 4 B, 4 A, 8 B, 4 A.

ROW 20: Ch 1, hdc in first 4 hdc, change to B, hdc in next 8 hdc, change to A, hdc in next 4 hdc, change to B, hdc in next 4 hdc, change to A, hdc across, turn—4 A, 8 B, 4 A, 4 B, 16 A.

ROW 21: Ch 1, hdc in first 16 hdc, change to B, hdc in next 4 hdc, change to A, hdc in next 3 hdc, 2 hdc in next hdc, late change to B, hdc-sc-tog, hdc in next 6 hdc, late change to A, hdc across, turn—16 A, 4 B, 6 A, 7 B, 3 A.

ROW 22: Ch 1, hdc in first 3 hdc, change to B, hdc in next 5 hdc, hdc-sc-tog, change to A, 2 hdc in next hdc, hdc in next 5 hdc, change to B, hdc in next 4 hdc, change to A, hdc across, turn—3 A, 6 B, 7 A, 4 B, 16 A.

ROW 23: Ch 1, hdc in first 16 hdc, change to B, hdc in next 4 hdc, change to A, hdc in next

6 hdc, 2 hdc in next hdc, late change to B, hdc-sc-tog, hdc in next 4 hdc, late change to A, hdc across, turn—16 A, 4 B, 9 A, 5 B, 2 A.

ROW 24: Ch 1, hdc in first 2 hdc, change to B, hdc in next 3 hdc, hdc-sc-tog, change to A, 2 hdc in next hdc, hdc in next 8 hdc, change to B, hdc in next 4 hdc, change to A, hdc across, turn—2 A, 4 B, 10 A, 4 B, 16 A.

ROW 25: Ch 1, hdc in first 16 hdc, change to B, hdc in next 4 hdc, change to A, hdc in next 10 hdc, 2 hdc in next hdc, late change to B, hdc-sc-tog, hdc in next hdc, change to A, hdc across, turn—16 A, 4 B, 13 A, 1 B, 2 A.

ROWS 26–30: Rep Row 2. Fasten off and weave in ends.

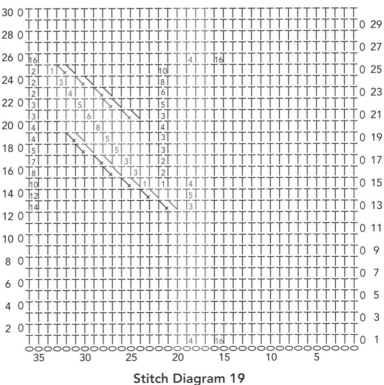

Stitch Diagram 19

Stem with Grass

Yarn Colors

A (#9758 Crypto Crystaline) and B (#9740 Seedling); see page 60 for further information.

Notes

- See Pattern Notes for All Squares on page 16.

- Remember, you can carry the unused color under just one stitch of another color. You can work most of Rows 11–12 with just one strand of B carried under the A stitches, while using a 1–2 yd (91.4 cm–1.8 m) length for each section of A.

- Refer to Stitch Diagram 20 on page 69 for assistance.

Pattern

With B, ch 37.

ROW 1: Hdc in second ch from hook and each ch across, turn—36 B.

ROWS 2–10: Ch 1, hdc in each hdc across, turn.

ROW 11: Ch 1, hdc in first 2 hdc, change to A, hdc in next hdc, change to B, hdc in next 4 hdc, change to A, hdc in next hdc, late change to B, hdc in next 2 hdc, [*change to A, hdc in next hdc, change to B, hdc in next 4 hdc*] twice, change to A, hdc in next hdc, late change to B, hdc in next 2 hdc, rep from * to *, [change to A, hdc in next hdc, change to B, hdc in next 2 hdc] twice, change to A, hdc in next hdc, change to B, hdc in next hdc, turn—2 B, 1 A, 4 B, 2 A, 1 B, 1 A, 4 B, 1 A, 4 B, 2 A, 1 B, 1 A, 4 B, 1 A, 2 B, 1 A, 2 B, 1 A, 1 B.

ROW 12: Ch 1, hdc in first hdc, change to A, hdc in next hdc, late change to B, hdc in next 2 hdc, [change to A, hdc in next hdc, change to B, hdc in next 2 hdc, change to A, hdc in next hdc, change to B, hdc in next hdc] twice, change to A, hdc in next 2 hdc, change to B, hdc in next 4 hdc, change to A, hdc in next hdc, change to B, hdc in next hdc, change to A, hdc in next hdc, late change to B, hdc in next 2 hdc, change to A, hdc in next hdc, change to B, hdc in next hdc, change to A, hdc in next 2 hdc, change to B, hdc in next 2 hdc, change to A, hdc in next hdc, late change to B, hdc in next hdc, change to A, hdc in next hdc, late change to B, hdc in next 2 hdc, turn—1 B, 2 A, 1 B, 1 A, 2 B, 1 A, 1 B, 1 A, 2 B, 1 A, 1 B, 2 A, 4 B, 1 A, 1 B, 2 A, 1 B, 1 A, 1 B, 2 A, 2 B, 4 A, 1 B.

ROW 13: Ch 1, hdc in first hdc, change to A, hdc in next 4 hdc, late change to B, hdc in next 2 hdc, change to A, *hdc in next 2 hdc, late change to B, hdc in next hdc, change to A, hdc in next hdc*, change to B, hdc in next hdc, change to A, rep from * to *, change to B, hdc in next 4 hdc, change to A, rep from * to *, late change to B, hdc in next hdc, late change to A, hdc in next 4 hdc, late change to B, hdc in next 2 hdc, change to A, hdc in next hdc, late change to B, hdc in next hdc, change to A, hdc across, turn—1 B, 5 A, 1 B, 4 A, 1 B, 4 A, 4 B, 5 A, 1 B, 4 A, 1 B, 5 A.

ROW 14: Ch 1, hdc in first 3 hdc, late change to B, hdc in next hdc, change to A, hdc in next 4 hdc, late change to B, hdc in next hdc, change to A, hdc in next 5 hdc, change to B, hdc in next 4 hdc, [change to A, hdc in next 4 hdc, late change to B, hdc in next hdc] twice, change to A, hdc in next 5 hdc, late change to B, hdc in next hdc, turn—16 A, 4 B, 16 A.

ROWS 15–30: Ch 1, hdc in first 16 hdc, change to B, hdc in next 4 hdc, change to A, hdc across, turn—16 A, 4 B, 16 A. Fasten off and weave in ends.

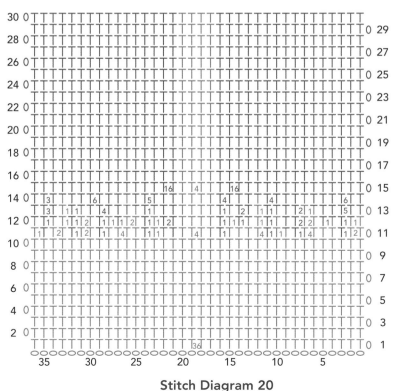

Stitch Diagram 20

Dragonfly

Yarn Colors

A (#9758 Crypto Crystaline), C (#9742 Pimpernel), D (#9764 Lidfors), and E (#9727 Spanish Brown); see page 60 for further information.

Notes

- See Pattern Notes for All Squares on page 16.
- Refer to Stitch Diagram 21 on page 71 for assistance.

Pattern

With A, ch 37.

ROW 1: Hdc in second ch from hook and each ch across, turn—36 A.

ROWS 2 AND 3: Ch 1, hdc in each hdc across, turn.

ROW 4: Ch 1, hdc in first 9 hdc, late change to E, 2 hdc in next hdc, late change to A, hdc-sc-tog, hdc across, turn—10 A, 2 E, 24 A.

ROW 5: Ch 1, hdc in first 22 hdc, hdc-sc-tog, change to E, hdc in next 2 hdc, change to A, 2 hdc in next hdc, hdc across, turn—23 A, 2 E, 11 A.

ROW 6: Ch 1, hdc in first 10 hdc, 2 hdc in next hdc, late change to E, hdc in next 2 hdc, late change to A, hdc-sc-tog, hdc across, turn—13 A, 2 E, 21 A.

ROW 7: Ch 1, hdc in first 19 hdc, hdc-sc-tog, change to E, hdc in next 2 hdc, change to A, 2 hdc in next hdc, hdc across, turn—20 A, 2 E, 14 A.

ROW 8: Ch 1, hdc in first 14 hdc, late change to E, hdc in next 2 hdc, late change to A, hdc across, turn—15 A, 2 E, 19 A.

ROW 9: Ch 1, hdc in first 19 hdc, change to E, hdc in next 2 hdc, change to A, hdc across, turn—19 A, 2 E, 15 A.

ROW 10: Ch 1, hdc in first 15 hdc, late change to E, hdc in next 2 hdc, late change to A, hdc across, turn—16 A, 2 E, 18 A.

ROW 11: Ch 1, hdc in first 3 hdc, hdc-sc-tog, change to D, 2 hdc in next hdc, hdc in next hdc, 2 hdc in next hdc, late change to A, hdc-sc-tog, hdc in next 8 hdc, change to E, hdc in next 2 hdc, change to A, hdc across, turn—4 A, 6 D, 8 A, 2 E, 16 A.

ROW 12: Ch 1, hdc in first 3 hdc, hdc-sc-tog, change to D, 2 hdc in next hdc, hdc in next 4 hdc, 2 hdc in next hdc, late change to A, hdc-sc-tog, hdc in next 3 hdc, late change to E, hdc in next 2 hdc, late change to A, hdc in next 5 hdc, hdc-sc-tog, change to D, 2 hdc in next hdc, hdc in next 6 hdc, late change to A, hdc across, turn—4 A, 9 D, 4 A, 2 E, 5 A, 9 D, 3 A.

ROW 13: Ch 1, hdc in first 3 hdc, change to D, hdc in next 9 hdc, 2 hdc in next hdc, late change to A, hdc-sc-tog, hdc in next 2 hdc, change to E, hdc in next 2 hdc, change to A, hdc in next hdc, hdc-sc-tog, change to D, 2 hdc in next hdc, hdc in next 9 hdc, 2 hdc in next hdc, late change to A, hdc-sc-tog, hdc in last hdc, turn—3 A, 12 D, 2 A, 2 E, 2 A, 14 D, 1 A.

ROW 14: Ch 1, hdc in first hdc, change to D, hdc in next 13 hdc, 2 hdc in next hdc, late change to A, hdc-sc-tog, change to E, hdc in next 2 hdc, change to A, hdc-sc-tog, change to D, 2 hdc in next hdc, hdc in next 9 hdc, hdc-sc-tog, change to A, 2 hdc in next hdc, hdc across, turn—1 A, 16 D, 2 E, 1 A, 12 D, 4 A.

ROW 15: Ch 1, hdc in first 4 hdc, late change to D, hdc in next 13 hdc, change to E, hdc in next 2 hdc, change to D, hdc in next 14 hdc, hdc-sc-tog, change to A, 2 hdc in last hdc, turn—5 A, 12 D, 2 E, 15 D, 2 A.

ROW 16: Ch 1, hdc in first 2 hdc, 2 hdc in next hdc, late change to D, hdc-sc-tog, hdc in next 12 hdc, change to E, hdc in next 2 hdc, change to D, hdc in next 9 hdc, hdc-sc-tog, change to A, 2 hdc in next hdc, hdc across, turn—5 A, 12 D, 2 E, 10 D, 7 A.

ROW 17: Ch 1, hdc in first 7 hdc, 2 hdc in next hdc, late change to D, hdc-sc-tog, hdc in next 7 hdc, change to E, hdc in next 2 hdc, change to D, hdc in next 10 hdc, hdc-sc-tog, change to A, 2 hdc in next hdc, hdc across, turn— 10 A, 7 D, 2 E, 11 D, 6 A.

ROW 18: Ch 1, hdc in first 10 hdc, hdc-sc-tog, change to C, 2 hdc in next hdc, hdc in next 4 hdc, change to E, hdc in next 2 hdc, change to C, hdc in next 3 hdc, 2 hdc in next hdc, late change to A, hdc-sc-tog, hdc across, turn— 11 A, 6 C, 2 E, 6 C, 11 A.

ROW 19: Ch 1, hdc in first 8 hdc, hdc-sc-tog, change to C, 2 hdc in next hdc, hdc in next 6 hdc, change to E, hdc in next 2 hdc, change to C, hdc in next 6 hdc, 2 hdc in next hdc, late change to A, hdc-sc-tog, hdc across, turn— 9 A, 8 C, 2 E, 9 C, 8 A.

ROW 20: Ch 1, hdc in first 6 hdc, hdc-sc-tog, change to C, 2 hdc in next hdc, hdc in next 8 hdc, change to E, hdc in next 2 hdc, change to C, hdc in next 8 hdc, 2 hdc in next hdc, late change to A, hdc-sc-tog, hdc across, turn— 7 A, 10 C, 2 E, 11 C, 6 A.

ROW 21: Ch 1, hdc in first 4 hdc, hdc-sc-tog, change to C, 2 hdc in next hdc, hdc in next 7 hdc, hdc-sc-tog, change to A, 2 hdc in next hdc, change to E, hdc-sc-tog, late change

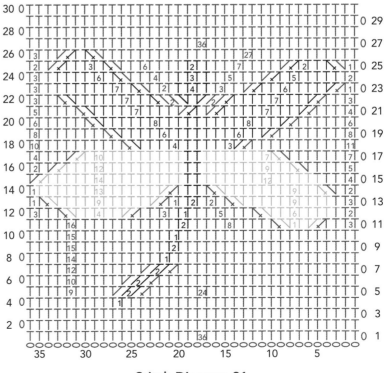

Stitch Diagram 21

to A, 2 hdc in next hdc, late change to C, hdc in next 8 hdc, 2 hdc in next hdc, late change to A, hdc-sc-tog, hdc across, turn—5 A, 10 C, 2 A, 2 E, 2 A, 10 C, 5 A.

ROW 22: Ch 1, hdc in first 3 hdc, hdc-sc-tog, change to C, 2 hdc in next hdc, hdc in next 7 hdc, hdc-sc-tog, change to A, hdc in next 2 hdc, change to E, 2 hdc in each of next 2 hdc, change to A, hdc in next 2 hdc, late change to C, hdc-sc-tog, hdc in next 7 hdc, 2 hdc in next hdc, late change to A, hdc-sc-tog, hdc across, turn—4 A, 10 C, 2 A, 4 E, 3 A, 10 C, 3 A.

ROW 23: Ch 1, hdc in first hdc, hdc-sc-tog, change to C, 2 hdc in next hdc, hdc in next 6 hdc, hdc-sc-tog, change to A, 2 hdc in next hdc, hdc in next 3 hdc, change to E, hdc in next 4 hdc, change to A, hdc in next 2 hdc, 2 hdc in next hdc, late change to C, hdc-sc-tog, hdc in next 7 hdc, late change to A, hdc across, turn—2 A, 9 C, 5 A, 4 E, 5 A, 8 C, 3 A.

ROW 24: Ch 1, hdc in first 3 hdc, change to C, hdc in next 6 hdc, hdc-sc-tog, change to A, 2 hdc in next hdc, hdc in next 4 hdc, late change to E, hdc in next 4 hdc, change to A, hdc in next 5 hdc, 2 hdc in next hdc, late change to C, hdc-sc-tog, hdc in next 6 hdc, change to A, hdc across, turn—3 A, 7 C, 7 A, 3 E, 8 A, 6 C, 2 A.

ROW 25: Ch 1, hdc in first hdc, 2 hdc in next hdc, late change to C, hdc-sc-tog, hdc in next 2 hdc, hdc-sc-tog, change to A, 2 hdc in next hdc, hdc in next 7 hdc, late change to E, hdc in next 3 hdc, change to A, hdc in next 6 hdc, 2 hdc in next hdc, late change to C, hdc-sc-tog, hdc in next 3 hdc, hdc-sc-tog, change to A, 2 hdc in next hdc, hdc across, turn— 4 A, 3 C, 10 A, 2 E, 9 A, 4 C, 4 A.

ROW 26: Ch 1, hdc in first 3 hdc, 2 hdc in next hdc, late change to C, 2 hdc-sc-tog, change to A, 2 hdc in next hdc, hdc across, turn—6 A, 1 C, 29 A.

ROWS 27–30: Rep Row 2. Fasten off and weave in ends.

PART 2:
Space-Themed Squares

The squares in this section were all designed as part of a blanket, made by a group of my friends for a little boy who was recovering from brain surgery. My own son helped to design the squares, sketching out space-themed images we thought the little boy would enjoy. He also helped to choose the colors he thought each of the designs should be made in. At the time, I had just begun work on this book, and I decided to include the space squares so that the book would have some options for boys. Although, of course, the little girl in your life may enjoy the space theme as well! Make all of the space squares, or just pick one or two to make an afghan for a special kiddo in your own life.

Yarn
Worsted weight (#4 Medium).

Shown Here: Berroco Comfort (50% super fine nylon, 50% super fine acrylic; 210 yd [193 m]/3.5 oz [100 g])

Color A: #9759 Duck Teal (blue)

Color B: #9740 Seedling (light green)

Color C: #9701 Ivory

Color D: #9742 Pimpernel (red)

Color E: #9729 Smokestack (light gray)

Color F: #9734 Liquorice (black)

(See Afghan Layouts for quantities for individual projects or estimate about 2 squares per 100 g ball.)

Important Notes and Reminders
- See Information for All Squares in Chapter 1 (page 16) for hook size, notions, gauge, pattern notes, and edging.

- Before completing the last stitch in the previous color, determine if you are making a late or regular color change. Remember, you will always carry the new color under the last stitch before a late color change when working in half double crochet.

- Remember to carry the new color under the 3 stitches before a color change on sharp angles.

Space Squares Color Key

■ Color A		■ Color D
■ Color B		■ Color E
■ Color C		■ Color F

SQUARE 22

Sun

Yarn Colors

A (#9758 Crypto Crystaline) and D (#9764 Lidfors); refer to page 60 for further information as the Sun square features colors used in the Garden-Themed section.

Notes

- See Pattern Notes for All Squares on page 16.
- Refer to Stitch Diagram 22 on page 75 for assistance.

Pattern

With A, ch 37.

ROW 1: Hdc in second ch from hook and each ch across, turn—36 A.

ROW 2: Ch 1, hdc in first 17 hdc, change to D, hdc in next hdc, late change to A, hdc across, turn—17 A, 2 D, 17 A.

ROW 3: Ch 1, hdc in first 17 hdc, change to D, hdc in next 2 hdc, change to A, hdc across, turn—17 A, 2 D, 17 A.

ROW 4: Ch 1, hdc in first 6 hdc, 2 hdc in next hdc, late change to D, hdc in next hdc, late change to A, hdc-sc-tog, hdc in next 7 hdc, change to D, hdc in next 2 hdc, late change to A, hdc in next 7 hdc, hdc-sc-tog, change to D, hdc in next hdc, change to A, 2 hdc in next hdc, hdc across, turn—9 A, 1 D, 7 A, 3 D, 7 A, 1 D, 8 A.

ROW 5: Ch 1, hdc in first 8 hdc, late change to D, 2 hdc in next hdc, late change to A, hdc-sc-tog, hdc in next 5 hdc, change to D, hdc in next 3 hdc, late change to A, hdc in next 5 hdc, hdc-sc-tog, change to D, 2 hdc in next hdc, change to A, hdc across, turn—9 A, 2 D, 5 A, 4 D, 5 A, 2 D, 9 A.

ROW 6: Ch 1, hdc in first 9 hdc, late change to D, hdc in next hdc, 2 hdc in next hdc, late change to A, hdc-sc-tog, hdc in next 3 hdc, change to D, hdc in next 4 hdc, late change to A, hdc in next 3 hdc, hdc-sc-tog, change to D, 2 hdc in next hdc, hdc in next hdc, change to A, hdc across, turn—10 A, 3 D, 3 A, 5 D, 3 A, 3 D, 9 A.

ROW 7: Ch 1, hdc in first 9 hdc, late change to D, hdc in next 2 hdc, 2 hdc in next hdc, late change to A, hdc-sc-tog, hdc in next hdc, change to D, hdc in next 5 hdc, late change to A, hdc in next hdc, hdc-sc-tog, change to D, 2 hdc in next hdc, hdc in next 2 hdc, change to A, hdc across, turn—10 A, 4 D, 1 A, 6 D, 1 A, 4 D, 10 A.

ROW 8: Ch 1, hdc in first 10 hdc, late change to D, hdc in next 16 hdc, change to A, hdc across, turn—11 A, 15 D, 10 A.

ROW 9: Ch 1, hdc in first 10 hdc, change to D, hdc in next 15 hdc, late change to A, hdc across, turn—10 A, 16 D, 10 A.

ROW 10: Ch 1, 2 hdc in first hdc, late change to D, hdc in next hdc, late change to A, hdc-sc-tog, hdc in next 4 hdc, hdc-sc-tog, change to D, 2 hdc in next hdc, hdc in next 14 hdc, 2 hdc in next hdc, late change to A, hdc-sc-tog, hdc in next 4 hdc, hdc-sc-tog, change to D, hdc in next hdc, change to A, 2 hdc in last hdc, turn—3 A, 1 D, 5 A, 19 D, 5 A, 1 D, 2 A.

ROW 11: Ch 1, hdc in first hdc, 2 hdc in next hdc, late change to D, hdc-sc-tog, hdc in next 27 hdc, hdc-sc-tog, change to A, 2 hdc in next hdc, hdc across, turn—4 A, 28 D, 4 A.

ROWS 12–14: Ch 1, hdc across to last A-color hdc, 2 hdc in next hdc, late change to D, hdc-sc-tog, hdc across to last 2 D-color hdc, hdc-sc-tog, change to A, 2 hdc in next hdc, hdc across, turn.

ROW 15: Ch 1, hdc in first 6 hdc, hdc-sc-tog, change to D, 2 hdc in next hdc, hdc in next 17 hdc, 2 hdc in next hdc, change to A, hdc-sc-tog, hdc across, turn—7 A, 21 D, 8 A.

ROW 16: Ch 1, hdc in first 6 hdc, 2 hdc in next hdc, change to D, hdc-sc-tog, hdc in next 18 hdc, hdc-sc-tog, late change to A, 2 hdc in next hdc, hdc across, turn—8 A, 21 D, 7 A.

ROWS 17–19: Ch 1, hdc across to last 2 A-color hdc, hdc-sc-tog, change to D, 2 hdc in next hdc, hdc across to last D-color hdc, 2 hdc in next hdc, late change to A, hdc-sc-tog, hdc across, turn.

ROW 20: Ch 1, hdc in first hdc, hdc-sc-tog, change to D, 2 hdc in next hdc, hdc in next 28 hdc, 2 hdc in next hdc, change to A, hdc-sc-tog, hdc in last hdc, turn—2 A, 32 D, 2 A.

ROW 21: Ch 1, hdc-sc-tog, late change to D, hdc in next hdc, *change to A, 2 hdc in next hdc, hdc in next 4 hdc, 2 hdc in next hdc, late change to D*, hdc-sc-tog, hdc in next 14 hdc, hdc-sc-tog, rep from * to *, hdc in next hdc, change to A, hdc-sc-tog, turn—11 A, 15 D, 10 A.

ROW 22: Rep Row 9.

ROW 23: Ch 1, hdc in first 10 hdc, change to D, hdc in next 16 hdc, late change to A, hdc across, turn—10 A, 17 D, 9 A.

ROW 24: Ch 1, hdc in first 9 hdc, change to D, hdc in next 2 hdc, hdc-sc-tog, change to A, 2 hdc in next hdc, hdc in next hdc, late change to D, hdc in next 5 hdc, change to A, hdc in next hdc, 2 hdc in next hdc, late change to D, hdc-sc-tog, hdc in next 2 hdc, late change to A, hdc across, turn—9 A, 3 D, 4 A, 4 D, 4 A, 3 D, 9 A.

ROW 25: Ch 1, hdc in first 9 hdc, change to D, hdc in next hdc, hdc-sc-tog, change to A, 2 hdc in next hdc, hdc in next 3 hdc, late

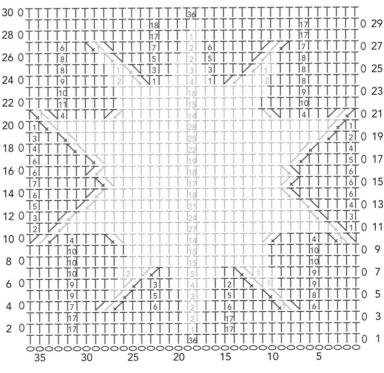

Stitch Diagram 22

change to D, hdc in next 4 hdc, change to A, hdc in next 3 hdc, 2 hdc in next hdc, late change to D, hdc-sc-tog, hdc in next hdc, late change to A, hdc across, turn—9 A, 2 D, 6 A, 3 D, 6 A, 2 D, 8 A.

ROW 26: Ch 1, hdc in first 8 hdc, change to D, hdc-sc-tog, change to A, 2 hdc in next hdc, hdc in next 5 hdc, late change to D, hdc in next 3 hdc, change to A, hdc in next 5 hdc, 2 hdc in next hdc, change to D, hdc-sc-tog, change to A, hdc across, turn—8 A, 1 D, 8 A, 2 D, 8 A, 1 D, 8 A.

ROW 27: Ch 1, hdc in first 7 hdc, hdc-sc-tog, late change to D, hdc in next hdc, change to A, 2 hdc in next hdc, hdc in next 6 hdc, change to D, hdc in next 2 hdc, change to A, hdc in next 7 hdc, 2 hdc in next hdc, late change to D, hdc in next hdc, change to A, hdc-sc-tog, hdc across, turn—17 A, 2 D, 17 A.

ROW 28: Ch 1, hdc in first 17 hdc, late change to D, hdc in next 2 hdc, change to A, hdc across, turn—17 A, 1 D, 18 A.

ROW 29: Ch 1, hdc in first 17 hdc, late change to D, hdc in next hdc, change to A, hdc across, turn—36 A.

ROW 30: Ch 1, hdc in each hdc across. Fasten off and weave in ends.

SQUARE
23 Moon

Yarn Colors

A (#9759 Duck Teal) and E (#9729 Smokestack); see page 73 for further information.

Notes

- See Pattern Notes for All Squares on page 16.

- Refer to Stitch Diagram 23 on page 77 for assistance.

Pattern

With A, ch 37.

ROW 1: Hdc in second ch from hook and each ch across, turn—36 A.

ROWS 2–4: Ch 1, hdc in each hdc across, turn.

ROW 5: Ch 1, hdc in first 11 hdc, hdc-sc-tog, change to E, 2 hdc in next hdc, hdc in next 4 hdc, 2 hdc in next hdc, late change to A, hdc-sc-tog, hdc across, turn—12 A, 9 E, 15 A.

ROW 6: Ch 1, hdc in first 12 hdc, hdc-sc-tog, change to E, 2 hdc in next hdc, hdc in next 9 hdc, 2 hdc in next hdc, late change to A, hdc-sc-tog, hdc across, turn—13 A, 14 E, 9 A.

ROW 7: Ch 1, hdc in first 6 hdc, hdc-sc-tog, change to E, 2 hdc in next hdc, hdc in next 14 hdc, 2 hdc in next hdc, late change to A, hdc-sc-tog, hdc across, turn—7 A, 19 E, 10 A.

ROW 8: Ch 1, hdc in first 8 hdc, hdc-sc-tog, change to E, 2 hdc in next hdc, hdc in next 17 hdc, 2 hdc in next hdc, late change to A, hdc-sc-tog, hdc across, turn—9 A, 22 E, 5 A.

ROW 9: Ch 1, hdc in first 9 hdc, 2 hdc in next hdc, late change to E, hdc-sc-tog, hdc in next 14 hdc, 2 hdc in next hdc, late change to A, hdc-sc-tog, hdc across, turn—12 A, 17 E, 7 A.

ROW 10: Ch 1, hdc in first 7 hdc, change to E, hdc in next 14 hdc, hdc-sc-tog, change to A, 2 hdc in next hdc, hdc across, turn—7 A, 15 E, 14 A.

ROW 11: Ch 1, hdc in first 14 hdc, 2 hdc in next hdc, late change to E, hdc-sc-tog, hdc in next 12 hdc, late change to A, hdc across, turn—17 A, 13 E, 6 A.

ROW 12: Ch 1, hdc in first 6 hdc, change to E, hdc in next 10 hdc, hdc-sc-tog, change to A, 2 hdc in next hdc, hdc across, turn—6 A, 11 E, 19 A.

ROW 13: Ch 1, hdc in first 18 hdc, 2 hdc in next hdc, late change to E, hdc-sc-tog, hdc in next 9 hdc, change to A, hdc across, turn—21 A, 9 E, 6 A.

ROW 14: Ch 1, hdc in each A-color hdc, change to E, hdc in each E-color hdc, change to A, hdc across, turn.

ROW 15: Ch 1, hdc in each A-color hdc, late change to E, hdc in each E-color hdc, change to A, hdc across, turn.

ROWS 16 AND 17: Rep Row 14.

ROWS 18 AND 19: Rep Rows 15 and 14.

ROW 20: Ch 1, hdc in each hdc to last A-color hdc, 2 hdc in next hdc, late change to E, hdc-sc-tog, hdc in each E-color hdc, late change to A, hdc across, turn.

ROW 21: Rep Row 14—20 A, 6 E, 10 A.

ROW 22: Rep Row 20—11 A, 5 E, 20 A.

ROW 23: Ch 1, hdc in each A-color hdc, change to E, hdc in each hdc to 2 last E-color hdc, hdc-sc-tog, change to A, 2 hdc in next hdc, hdc across, turn.

ROWS 24 AND 25: Rep Rows 20 and 23.

ROW 26: Ch 1, hdc in first 14 hdc, 2 hdc in next hdc, late change to E, hdc-sc-tog, change to A, hdc across, turn—36 A.

ROWS 27–30: Ch 1, hdc in each hdc across, turn. Fasten off and weave in ends.

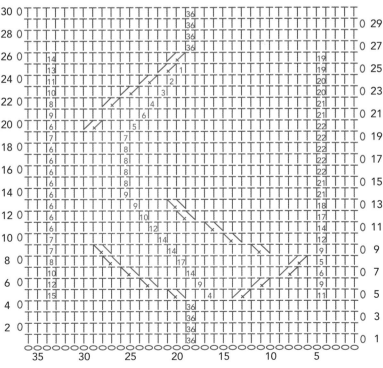

Stitch Diagram 23

SQUARE 24

Ringed Planet

Yarn Colors

A (#9759 Duck Teal), B (#9740 Seedling), and D (#9742 Pimpernel); see page 73 for further information.

Notes

- See Pattern Notes for All Squares on page 16.
- Refer to Stitch Diagram 24 on page 79 for assistance.

Pattern

With A, ch 37.

ROW 1: Hdc in second ch from hook and each ch across, turn—36 A.

Rows 2–7: Ch 1, hdc in each hdc across, turn.

ROW 8: Ch 1, hdc in first 14 hdc, hdc-sc-tog, change to B, 2 hdc in next hdc, hdc in next 2 hdc, 2 hdc in next hdc, late change to A, hdc-sc-tog, hdc across, turn—15 A, 7 B, 14 A.

ROW 9: Ch 1, hdc in first 12 hdc, hdc-sc-tog, change to B, 2 hdc in next hdc, hdc in next 5 hdc, 2 hdc in next hdc, late change to A, hdc-sc-tog, hdc across, turn—13 A, 10 B, 13 A.

ROW 10: Ch 1, hdc in first 11 hdc, hdc-sc-tog, change to B, 2 hdc in next hdc, hdc in next 8 hdc, 2 hdc in next hdc, late change to A, hdc-sc-tog, hdc across, turn—12 A, 13 B, 11 A.

ROW 11: Ch 1, hdc in first 11 hdc, change to B, hdc in next 13 hdc, late change to A, hdc across, turn—11 A, 14 B, 11 A.

ROW 12: Ch 1, hdc in first 7 hdc, hdc-sc-tog, change to E, 2 hdc in next hdc, hdc in next 16 hdc, 2 hdc in next hdc, late change to A, hdc-sc-tog, hdc across, turn—8 A, 21 E, 7 A.

ROW 13: Ch 1, hdc in first 4 hdc, hdc-sc-tog, change to E, 2 hdc in next hdc, hdc in next 21 hdc, 2 hdc in next hdc, late change to A, hdc-sc-tog, hdc across, turn—5 A, 26 E, 5 A.

ROW 14: Ch 1, hdc in first 2 hdc, hdc-sc-tog, change to E, 2 hdc in next hdc, hdc in next 3 hdc, hdc-sc-tog, change to A, hdc in next hdc, change to B, hdc in same hdc, hdc in next 15 hdc, late change to A, hdc in same hdc, late change to E, hdc-sc-tog, hdc in next 3 hdc, 2 hdc in next hdc, late change to A, hdc-sc-tog, hdc across, turn—3 A, 6 E, 1 A, 17 B, 1 A, 6 E, 2 A.

ROW 15: Ch 1, hdc-sc-tog, change to E, 2 hdc in next hdc, hdc in next 2 hdc, hdc-sc-tog, change to A, 2 hdc in next hdc, hdc in next hdc, change to B, hdc in next 17 hdc, late change to A, hdc in next hdc, 2 hdc in next hdc, late change to E, hdc-sc-tog, hdc in next 3 hdc, 2 hdc in next hdc, change to A, hdc-sc-tog, turn—1 A, 5 E, 3 A, 18 B, 3 A, 5 E, 1 A.

ROW 16: Ch 1, hdc in first hdc, late change to E, hdc in next 5 hdc, late change to A, hdc in next 3 hdc, late change to B, hdc in next 18 hdc, change to A, hdc in next 3 hdc, change to E, hdc in next 5 hdc, change to A, hdc in next hdc, turn—2 A, 5 E, 3 A, 17 B, 3 A, 5 E, 1 A.

ROW 17: Ch 1, 2 hdc in first hdc, late change to E, hdc-sc-tog, hdc in next 2 hdc, 2 hdc in next hdc, late change to A, hdc-sc-tog, hdc in next hdc, late change to B, hdc in next 17 hdc, change to A, hdc in next hdc, hdc-sc-tog, change to E, 2 hdc in next hdc, hdc in next 2 hdc, hdc-sc-tog, change to A, 2 hdc in next hdc, hdc in last hdc, turn—3 A, 5 E, 2 A, 16 B, 2 A, 5 E, 2 A.

ROW 18: Ch 1, hdc in first 2 hdc, 2 hdc in next hdc, late change to E, hdc-sc-tog, hdc in next 3 hdc, 2 hdc in next hdc, late change to A, hdc in next hdc, change to B, hdc-sc-tog, hdc in next 14 hdc, change to A, hdc in next hdc, change to E, hdc in next 4 hdc, hdc-sc-tog, change to A, 2 hdc in next hdc, hdc in next 2 hdc, turn—5 A, 6 E, 15 B, 1 A, 5 E, 4 A.

ROW 19: Ch 1, hdc in first 4 hdc, 2 hdc in next hdc, late change to E, hdc-sc-tog, hdc in next 3 hdc, late change to B, hdc in next 15 hdc, change to E, hdc in next 4 hdc, hdc-sc-tog, change to A, 2 hdc in next hdc, hdc across, turn—7 A, 4 E, 14 B, 5 E, 6 A.

ROW 20: Ch 1, hdc in first 7 hdc, 2 hdc in next hdc, late change to E, hdc-sc-tog, hdc in next hdc, late change to B, hdc in next 14 hdc, change to E, hdc in next hdc, hdc-sc-tog, change to A, 2 hdc in next hdc, hdc across, turn—10 A, 2 E, 13 B, 2 E, 9 A.

ROW 21: Ch 1, hdc in first 11 hdc, late change to B, hdc in next 13 hdc, change to A, hdc across, turn—12 A, 12 B, 12 A.

ROW 22: Ch 1, hdc in first 11 hdc, 2 hdc in next hdc, late change to B, hdc-sc-tog, hdc in next 8 hdc, hdc-sc-tog, change to A, 2 hdc in next hdc, hdc across, turn—14 A, 9 B, 13 A.

ROW 23: Ch 1, hdc in first 12 hdc, 2 hdc in next hdc, late change to B, hdc-sc-tog, hdc in next 5 hdc, hdc-sc-tog, change to A, 2 hdc in next hdc, hdc across, turn—15 A, 6 B, 15 A.

ROW 24: Ch 1, hdc in first 14 hdc, 2 hdc in next hdc, late change to B, hdc-sc-tog, hdc in next 2 hdc, hdc-sc-tog, change to A, 2 hdc in next hdc, hdc across, turn—17 A, 3 B, 16 A.

ROWS 25–30: Ch 1, hdc in each hdc across, turn. Fasten off and weave in ends.

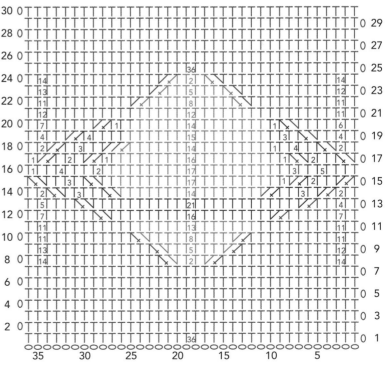

Stitch Diagram 24

Rocket

Yarn Colors

A (#9759 Duck Teal), C (#9701 Ivory), D (#9742 Pimpernel), E (#9729 Smokestack), and F (#9734 Liquorice); see page 73 for further information.

Notes

- See Pattern Notes for All Squares on page 16.
- Refer to Stitch Diagram 25 on page 81.

Pattern

With A, ch 37.

ROW 1: Hdc in second ch from hook and each ch across, turn—36 A.

ROW 2: Ch 1, hdc in each hdc across, turn.

ROW 3: Ch 1, hdc in first 14 hdc, *change to D, hdc in next hdc, late change to A*, hdc in next 2 hdc, rep from * to *, hdc in next 4 hdc, rep from * to *, hdc across, turn—14 A, 2 D, 1 A, 2 D, 3 A, 2 D, 12 A.

ROW 4: Ch 1, hdc in first 4 hdc, change to F, hdc in next hdc, late change to A, hdc in next 7 hdc, *change to D, hdc in next 2 hdc, late change to A, hdc in next hdc, change to E*, hdc in next hdc, late change to A, hdc in next hdc, rep from * to *, hdc in next 2 hdc, late change to A, hdc in next 9 hdc, change to F, hdc in next hdc, change to A, hdc across, turn—4 A, 2 F, 6 A, 11 D, 8 A, 1 F, 4 A.

ROW 5: Ch 1, hdc in first 4 hdc, late change to F, 2 hdc in next hdc, late change to A, hdc-sc-tog, hdc in next 4 hdc, hdc-sc-tog, change to D, 2 hdc in next hdc, hdc in next 10 hdc, change to A, hdc in next 4 hdc, hdc-sc-tog, change to F, hdc in next 2 hdc, change to A, 2 hdc in next hdc, hdc across, turn—5 A, 2 F, 5 A, 12 D, 5 A, 2 F, 5 A.

ROW 6: Ch 1, hdc in first 5 hdc, late change to F, hdc in next hdc, 2 hdc in next hdc, late change to A, hdc-sc-tog, hdc in next 3 hdc, change to E, hdc in next 12 hdc, change to A, hdc in next 3 hdc, hdc-sc-tog, change to F, 2 hdc in next hdc, hdc in next hdc, change to A, hdc across, turn—6 A, 3 F, 3 A, 12 E, 4 A, 3 F, 5 A.

ROW 7: Ch 1, hdc in first 5 hdc, late change to F, hdc in next 2 hdc, 2 hdc in next hdc, late change to A, hdc-sc-tog, hdc in next 2 hdc, change to E, hdc in next 2 hdc, change to F, hdc in next 4 hdc, change to E, hdc in next 6 hdc, change to A, hdc in next hdc, hdc-sc-tog, change to F, 2 hdc in next hdc, hdc in next 2 hdc, change to A, hdc across, turn—6 A, 4 F, 2 A, 2 E, 4 F, 6 E, 2 A, 4 F, 6 A.

ROW 8: Ch 1, hdc in first 6 hdc, late change to F, hdc in next 3 hdc, 2 hdc in next hdc, late change to A, hdc-sc-tog, change to E, hdc in next 6 hdc, change to F, hdc in next 4 hdc, change to E, hdc in next 2 hdc, change to A, hdc-sc-tog, change to F, 2 hdc in next hdc, hdc in next 3 hdc, change to A, hdc across, turn—7 A, 5 F, 6 E, 4 F, 2 E, 1 A, 5 F, 6 A.

ROW 9: Ch 1, hdc in first 6 hdc, late change to F, hdc in next 6 hdc, change to E, hdc in next 2 hdc, change to F, hdc in next 4 hdc, change to E, hdc in next 6 hdc, change to F, hdc in next 5 hdc, change to A, hdc across, turn—7 A, 5 F, 2 E, 4 F, 6 E, 5 F, 7 A.

ROW 10: Ch 1, hdc in first 7 hdc, late change to F, hdc in next 5 hdc, change to E, hdc in next 6 hdc, change to F, hdc in next 4 hdc, change to E, hdc in next 2 hdc, change to F, hdc in next 3 hdc, hdc-sc-tog, change to A, 2 hdc in next hdc, hdc across, turn—8 A, 4 F, 6 E, 4 F, 2 E, 4 F, 8 A.

ROW 11: Ch 1, hdc in first 8 hdc, late change to F, hdc in next 4 hdc, change to E, hdc in next hdc, 2 hdc in next hdc, late change to F, 2 hdc-sc-tog, change to E, 2 hdc in next hdc, hdc in next 5 hdc, change to F, hdc in next 2 hdc, hdc-sc-tog, change to A, 2 hdc in next hdc, hdc across, turn—9 A, 3 F, 4 E, 1 F, 7 E, 3 F, 9 A.

ROW 12: Ch 1, hdc in first 8 hdc, 2 hdc in next hdc, late change to F, hdc-sc-tog, hdc in next hdc, change to E, hdc in next 12 hdc, change to F, hdc in next hdc, hdc-sc-tog, change to A, 2 hdc in next hdc, hdc across, turn—11 A, 1 F, 12 E, 2 F, 10 A.

ROWS 13–15: Ch 1, hdc in first 12 hdc, change to E, hdc in next 12 hdc, change to A, hdc across, turn—12 A, 12 E, 12 A.

ROW 16: Ch 1, hdc in first 12 hdc, change to E, hdc in next 2 hdc, hdc-sc-tog, change to C, 2 hdc in next hdc, hdc in next hdc, 2 hdc in next hdc, late change to E, hdc-sc-tog, hdc in next 3 hdc, change to A, hdc across, turn—12 A, 3 E, 6 C, 3 E, 12 A.

ROW 17: Ch 1, hdc in first 12 hdc, change to E, hdc in next 3 hdc, change to C, hdc in next 6 hdc, change to E, hdc in next 3 hdc, change to A, hdc across, turn—12 A, 3 E, 6 C, 3 E, 12 A.

ROW 18: Ch 1, hdc in first 12 hdc, late change to E, hdc in next 3 hdc, late change to C, hdc in next 6 hdc, change to E, hdc in next 3 hdc, change to A, hdc across, turn—13 A, 3 E, 5 C, 3 E, 12 A.

ROW 19: Ch 1, hdc in first 12 hdc, late change to E, hdc in next 2 hdc, 2 hdc in next hdc, late change to C, hdc-sc-tog, hdc in next hdc, hdc-sc-tog, change to E, 2 hdc in next hdc, hdc in next 2 hdc, change to A, hdc across, turn—13 A, 4 E, 2 C, 4 E, 13 A.

ROW 20: Ch 1, hdc in first 13 hdc, late change to E, hdc in next 10 hdc, change to A, hdc across, turn—14 A, 9 E, 13 A.

ROWS 21–26: Ch 1, hdc in each A-color hdc, late change to E, hdc in each E-color hdc, change to A, hdc across, turn.

ROW 27: Ch 1, hdc in first 15 hdc, 2 hdc in next hdc, late change to E, hdc-sc-hdc-tog, change to A, 2 hdc in next hdc, hdc across, turn—36 A.

ROWS 28–30: Ch 1, hdc in each hdc across, turn. Fasten off and weave in ends.

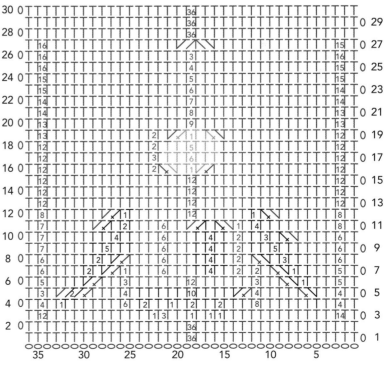

Stitch Diagram 25

26

UFO

To avoid extra B yarn ends, carry B yarn under the bottoms and over the tops of the D stitches (see Bridging Over on page 135).

Yarn Colors

A (#9759 Duck Teal), B (#9740 Seedling), C (#9701 Ivory), and D (#9742 Pimpernel); see page 73 for further information.

Notes

- See Pattern Notes for All Squares on page 16.
- Refer to Stitch Diagram 26 on page 83 for assistance.

Pattern

With A, ch 37.

ROW 1: Hdc in second ch from hook and each ch across, turn—36 A.

Rows 2–6: Ch 1, hdc in each hdc across, turn.

ROW 7: Ch 1, hdc in first 13 hdc, hdc-sc-tog, change to B, 2 hdc in next hdc, hdc in next 4 hdc, 2 hdc in next hdc, late change to A, hdc-sc-tog, hdc across, turn—14 A, 9 B, 13 A.

ROW 8: Ch 1, hdc in first 10 hdc, hdc-sc-tog, change to B, 2 hdc in next hdc, hdc in next 9 hdc, 2 hdc in next hdc, late change to A, hdc-sc-tog, hdc across, turn—11 A, 14 B, 11 A.

ROW 9: Ch 1, hdc in first 8 hdc, hdc-sc-tog, change to B, 2 hdc in next hdc, hdc in next 4 hdc, hdc-sc-tog, change to D, 2 hdc in next 2 hdc, change to B, hdc-sc-tog, hdc in next 4 hdc, 2 hdc in next hdc, late change to A, hdc-sc-tog, hdc across, turn—9 A, 7 B, 4 D, 8 B, 8 A.

ROW 10: Ch 1, hdc in first 5 hdc, hdc-sc-tog, change to B, hdc in next 4 hdc, change to D, 2 hdc in next 2 hdc, change to B, hdc in next 2 hdc, late change to D, hdc-sc-tog, hdc in next hdc, hdc-sc-tog, change to B, hdc in next 2 hdc, change to D, 2 hdc in next 2 hdc, change to B, hdc in next 4 hdc, late change to A, hdc-sc-tog, hdc across, turn—6 A, 4 B, 4 D, 3 B, 2 D, 2 B, 4 D, 5 B, 6 A.

ROW 11: Ch 1, hdc in first 3 hdc, hdc-sc-tog, change to B, hdc in next 2 hdc, change to D, 2 hdc in next 2 hdc, change to B, hdc in next hdc, *late change to D, hdc-sc-tog, hdc in next hdc, hdc-sc-tog, change to B*, 2 hdc in next hdc, in next 4 hdc, 2 hdc in next hdc, rep from * to *, hdc in next hdc, change to D, 2 hdc in next 2 hdc, change to B, hdc in next 2 hdc, late change to A, hdc-sc-tog, hdc across, turn—4 A, 2 B, 4 D, 2 B, 2 D, 9 B, 2 D, 1 B, 4 D, 3 B, 3 A.

ROW 12: Ch 1, hdc in first hdc, hdc-sc-tog, change to B, 2 hdc in next 2 hdc, *late change to D, hdc-sc-tog, hdc in next hdc, hdc-sc-tog, change to B, 2 hdc in next hdc*, hdc in next 13 hdc, 2 hdc in next hdc, rep from * to *, 2 hdc in next 2 hdc, late change to A, hdc-sc-tog, hdc across, turn—2 A, 5 B, 2 D, 18 B, 2 D, 5 B, 2 A.

ROW 13: Ch 1, hdc in first 2 hdc, late change to B, hdc in next 32 hdc, change to A, hdc across, turn—3 A, 31 B, 2 A.

ROW 14: Ch 1, hdc in first 2 hdc, 2 hdc in next hdc, late change to B, hdc-sc-tog, hdc in next 25 hdc, hdc-sc-tog, change to A, 2 hdc in next hdc, hdc across, turn—5 A, 26 B, 5 A.

ROW 15: Ch 1, hdc in first 10 hdc, change to B, hdc in next 6 hdc, change to C, hdc in next 4 hdc, change to B, hdc in next 6 hdc, change to A, hdc across, turn—10 A, 6 B, 4 C, 6 B, 10 A.

ROWS 16–18: Ch 1, hdc in first 10 hdc, change to C, hdc in next 3 hdc, change to B, hdc in next 3 hdc, change to C, hdc in next 4 hdc, change to B, hdc in next 3 hdc, change to C, hdc in next 3 hdc, change to A, hdc across, turn—10 A, 3 C, 3 B, 4 C, 3 B, 3 C, 10 A.

ROW 19: Ch 1, hdc in first 10 hdc, change to C, hdc in next 3 hdc, change to B, hdc in next 2 hdc, 2 hdc in next hdc, late change to C, 2 hdc-sc-tog, change to B, 2 hdc in next hdc, hdc in next 2 hdc, change to C, hdc in next 3 hdc, change to A, hdc across, turn—10 A, 3 C, 5 B, 1 C, 4 B, 3 C, 10 A.

ROW 20: Ch 1, hdc in first 10 hdc, change to C, hdc in next hdc, hdc-sc-tog, change to B, 2 hdc in next hdc, hdc in next 8 hdc, 2 hdc in next hdc, late change to C, hdc-sc-tog, hdc in next hdc, change to A, hdc across, turn—10 A, 2 C, 13 B, 1 C, 10 A.

ROW 21: Ch 1, hdc in first 10 hdc, change to B, hdc in next 16 hdc, change to A, hdc across, turn—10 A, 16 B, 10 A.

ROW 22: Ch 1, hdc in first 9 hdc, 2 hdc in next hdc, late change to B, hdc-sc-tog, hdc in next 12 hdc, hdc-sc-tog, change to A, 2 hdc in next hdc, hdc across, turn—12 A, 13 B, 11 A.

ROW 23: Ch 1, hdc in first 10 hdc, 2 hdc in next hdc, late change to B, hdc-sc-tog, hdc in next 9 hdc, hdc-sc-tog, change to A, 2 hdc in next hdc, hdc across, turn—13 A, 10 B, 13 A.

ROW 24: Ch 1, hdc in first 12 hdc, 2 hdc in next hdc, late change to B, hdc-sc-tog, hdc in next 6 hdc, hdc-sc-tog, change to A, 2 hdc in next hdc, hdc across, turn—15 A, 7 B, 14 A.

ROWS 25–30: Ch 1, hdc in each hdc across, turn. Fasten off and weave in ends.

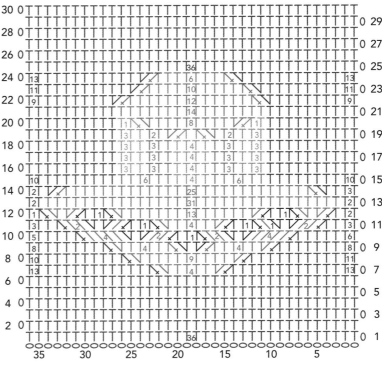

Stitch Diagram 26

Alien

Yarn Colors

A (#9759 Duck Teal), B (#9740 Seedling), C (#9701 Ivory), and D (#9742 Pimpernel); see page 73 for further information.

Notes

- See Pattern Notes for All Squares on page 16.
- Refer to Stitch Diagram 27 on page 85 for assistance.

Pattern

With A, ch 37.

ROW 1: Hdc in second ch from hook and each ch across, turn—36 A.

ROW 2: Ch 1, hdc in each hdc across, turn.

ROW 3: Ch 1, hdc in first 9 hdc, *hdc-sc-tog, change to B, 2 hdc in next 2 hdc, late change to A, hdc-sc-tog*, hdc in next 6 hdc, rep from * to *, hdc across, turn—10 A, 5 B, 7 A, 5 B, 9 A.

ROW 4: Ch 1, hdc in first 2 hdc, *hdc-sc-tog, change to B, 2 hdc in next 2 hdc, late change to A, hdc-sc-tog*, hdc in next hdc, late change to B, hdc in next 5 hdc, late change to A, hdc in next 7 hdc, change to B, hdc in next 5 hdc, change to A, hdc in next hdc, rep from * to *, hdc across, turn—3 A, 5 B, 2 A, 5 B, 6 A, 5 B, 2 A, 5 B, 3 A.

Rows 5 and 6: Ch 1, [hdc in each A-color hdc, late change to B, hdc in next 5 hdc, late change to A] twice, [hdc in each A-color hdc, change to B, hdc in next 5 hdc, change to A] twice, hdc across, turn.

ROW 7: Ch 1, hdc in first 3 hdc, 2 hdc in next hdc, late change to B, hdc-sc-tog, hdc in next 2 hdc, 2 hdc in next hdc, late change to A, hdc-sc-tog, late change to B, hdc in next 5 hdc, late change to A, hdc in next 4 hdc, change to B, hdc in next 5 hdc, change to A, hdc-sc-tog, change to B, 2 hdc in next hdc, hdc in next 2 hdc, hdc-sc-tog, change to A, 2 hdc in next hdc, hdc across, turn—6 A, 5 B, 1 A, 5 B, 3 A, 5 B, 1 A, 5 B, 5 A.

ROW 8: Rep Row 5—6 A, 5 B, 1 A, 5 B, 2 A, 5 B, 1 A, 5 B, 6 A.

ROW 9: Ch 1, hdc in first 5 hdc, 2 hdc in next hdc, late change to B, hdc-sc-tog, hdc in next 3 hdc, late change to A, hdc in next hdc, late change to B, hdc in next 5 hdc, late change to A, hdc in next 2 hdc, change to B, hdc in next 5 hdc, change to A, hdc in next hdc, change to B, hdc in next 3 hdc, hdc-sc-tog, change to A, 2 hdc in next hdc, hdc across, turn—8 A, 4 B, 1 A, 5 B, 1 A, 5 B, 1 A, 4 B, 7 A.

ROW 10: Ch 1, hdc in first 6 hdc, 2 hdc in next hdc, late change to B, hdc-sc-tog, hdc in next hdc, 2 hdc in next hdc, late change to A, hdc in next hdc, late change to B, hdc-sc-tog, hdc in next 3 hdc, late change to A, hdc in next hdc, change to B, hdc in next 3 hdc, hdc-sc-tog, change to A, hdc in next hdc, change to B, 2 hdc in next hdc, hdc in next hdc, hdc-sc-tog, change to A, 2 hdc in next hdc, hdc across, turn—9 A, 4 B, 1 A, 8 B, 1 A, 4 B, 9 A.

ROW 11: Ch 1, hdc in first 8 hdc, 2 hdc in next hdc, late change to B, hdc-sc-tog, hdc in next hdc, 2 hdc in next hdc, late change to A, hdc in next hdc, change to B, hdc-sc-tog, hdc in next 4 hdc, hdc-sc-tog, late change to A, hdc in next hdc, change to B, 2 hdc in next hdc, hdc in next hdc, hdc-sc-tog, change to A, 2 hdc in next hdc, hdc across, turn—11 A, 15 B, 10 A.

ROWS 12 AND 13: Ch 1, hdc in each hdc to last A-color hdc, 2 hdc in next hdc, late change to B, hdc-sc-tog, hdc in each hdc to last 2 B-color hdc, hdc-sc-tog, change to A, 2 hdc in next hdc, hdc across, turn.

ROW 14: Ch 1, hdc in first 12 hdc, 2 hdc in next hdc, change to B, hdc-sc-tog, hdc in next 7 hdc, change to A, hdc across, turn—14 A, 8 B, 14 A.

ROW 15: Ch 1, hdc in first 14 hdc, change to B, hdc in next 8 hdc, change to A, hdc across, turn—14 A, 8 B, 14 A.

ROWS 16 AND 17: Ch 1, hdc in each A-color hdc, change to B, hdc in each B-color hdc, late change to A, hdc across, turn.

ROW 18: Ch 1, hdc in first 13 hdc, change to B, hdc in next 3 hdc, change to C, hdc in next hdc, late change to B, hdc in next 6 hdc, late change to A, hdc across, turn—13 A, 3 B, 2 C, 6 B, 12 A.

ROW 19: Ch 1, hdc in first 12 hdc, change to B, hdc in next 2 hdc, change to C, 2 hdc in next hdc, change to B, hdc-sc-tog, hdc in next hdc, change to C, hdc in next 2 hdc, change to B, hdc in next 3 hdc, late change to A, hdc across, turn—12 A, 2 B, 2 C, 2 B, 2 C, 4 B, 12 A.

ROW 20: Ch 1, hdc in first 12 hdc, change to B, hdc in next 4 hdc, change to C, hdc in next 2 hdc, change to B, hdc in next 2 hdc, change to C, hdc in next 2 hdc, change to B, hdc in next 2 hdc, late change to A, hdc across, turn—12 A, 4 B, 2 C, 2 B, 2 C, 3 B, 11 A.

ROW 21: Ch 1, hdc in first 11 hdc, change to B, hdc in next 13 hdc, change to A, hdc across, turn—11 A, 13 B, 12 A.

ROW 22: Ch 1, hdc in first 12 hdc, change to B, hdc in next hdc, hdc-sc-tog, change to C, 2 hdc in each of next 2 hdc, change to B, hdc-sc-tog, hdc in next hdc, hdc-sc-tog, change to C, 2 hdc in next hdc, hdc in next hdc, change to B, hdc in same hdc as last hdc, hdc in next hdc, change to A, hdc-sc-tog, hdc across, turn—12 A, 2 B, 4 C, 3 B, 3 C, 2 B, 10 A.

ROW 23: Ch 1, hdc in first 10 hdc, change to B, hdc in next 2 hdc, late change to C, hdc in next hdc, hdc-sc-tog, change to B, 2 hdc in next hdc, hdc in next 2 hdc, late change to C, hdc in next 4 hdc, change to B, hdc in next 2 hdc, change to A, hdc across, turn—10 A, 3 B, 1 C, 5 B, 3 C, 2 B, 12 A.

ROW 24: Ch 1, hdc in first 12 hdc, change to B, hdc in next hdc, 2 hdc in next hdc, late change to C, hdc-sc-tog, hdc in next hdc, change to B, hdc in next 7 hdc, hdc-sc-tog, change to A, 2 hdc in next

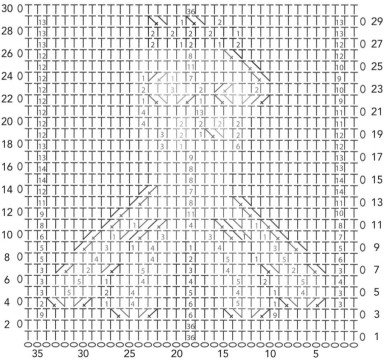

Stitch Diagram 27

hdc, hdc across, turn—12 A, 4 B, 1 C, 8 B, 11 A.

ROW 25: Ch 1, hdc in first 11 hdc, late change to D, hdc in same hdc, late change to B, hdc-sc-tog, hdc in next 11 hdc, change to A, hdc across, turn—12 A, 1 D, 11 B, 12 A.

ROW 26: Ch 1, hdc in first 12 hdc, late change to B, hdc in next 9 hdc, hdc-sc-tog, change to D, 2 hdc in next hdc, change to A, hdc across, turn—13 A, 9 B, 2 D, 12 A.

ROW 27: Ch 1, hdc in first 12 hdc, [late change to D, hdc in next 3 hdc, change to A, hdc in next hdc] 3 times, hdc across, turn—13 A, 2 D, 2 A, 2 D, 2 A, 2 D, 13A.

ROW 28: Ch 1, hdc in first 13 hdc, [change to D, hdc in next 2 hdc, change to A, hdc in next 2 hdc] twice, late change to D, hdc in next 2 hdc, change to A, hdc across, turn—13 A, 2 D, 2 A, 2 D, 3 A, 1 D, 13 A.

ROW 29: Ch 1, hdc in first 13 hdc, late change to D, hdc in next hdc, change to A, hdc in next 2 hdc, [2 hdc in next hdc, late change to D, hdc-sc-tog, change to A, hdc in next hdc] twice, hdc across, turn—36 A.

ROW 30: Ch 1, hdc in each hdc across, turn. Fasten off and weave in all ends.

SQUARE
28

Tip
To save ends, you can carry the D yarn under the B-color stitches between the two parts of the antennae on the sides of the robot's head. You will be embroidering over those stitches to form the antennae, so the yarn color will blend in with the embroidery stitches.

Robot

Yarn Colors
A (#9759 Duck Teal), B (#9740 Seedling), C (#9701 Ivory), D (#9742 Pimpernel), E (#9729 Smokestack), and F (#9734 Liquorice); see page 73 for further information.

Notes
- See Pattern Notes for All Squares on page 16.
- Refer to Stitch Diagram 28 on page 87 for assistance.

Pattern

With A, ch 37.

ROW 1: Hdc in second ch from hook and each ch across, turn—36 A.

ROW 2: Ch 1, hdc in each hdc across, turn.

ROW 3: Ch 1, hdc in first 9 hdc, *change to F, hdc in next 6 hdc, change to A*, hdc in next 6 hdc, rep from * to *, hdc across, turn—9 A, 6 F, 6 A, 6 F, 9 A.

ROW 4: Ch 1, hdc in first 9 hdc, *late change to F, hdc in next 6 hdc, change to A*, hdc in next 6 hdc, rep from * to *, hdc across, turn—10 A, 5 F, 7 A, 5 F, 9 A.

ROW 5: Ch 1, hdc in first 9 hdc, *late change to F, hdc in next 5 hdc, change to A*, hdc in next 7 hdc, rep from * to *, hdc across, turn—10 A, 4 F, 8 A, 4 F, 10 A.

Rows 6–8: Ch 1, hdc in first 10 hdc, *change to E, hdc in next 4 hdc, change to A*, hdc in next 8 hdc, rep from * to *, hdc across, turn—10 A, 4 E, 8 A, 4 E, 10 A.

ROW 9: Ch 1, hdc in first 10 hdc, late change to E, hdc in next 4 hdc, late change to A, hdc in next 8 hdc, change to E, hdc in next 4 hdc, change to A, hdc across, turn—11 A, 4 E, 7 A, 4 E, 10 A.

ROW 10: Ch 1, hdc in first 10 hdc, late change to E, hdc in next 4 hdc, change to A, hdc in next 7 hdc, change to E, hdc in next 4 hdc, change to A, hdc across, turn—11 A, 3 E, 7 A, 4 E, 11 A.

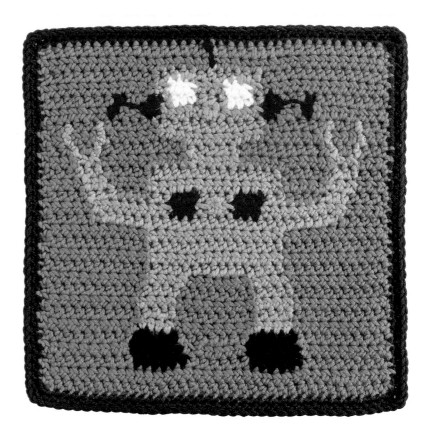

ROWS 11–14: Ch 1, hdc in first 11 hdc, change to E, hdc in next 14 hdc, change to A, hdc across, turn—11 A, 14 E, 11 A.

ROW 15: Ch 1, hdc in first 4 hdc, hdc-sc-tog, change to E, 2 hdc in next hdc, hdc in next 22 hdc, 2 hdc in next hdc, late change to A, hdc-sc-tog, hdc across, turn—5 A, 27 E, 4 A.

ROW 16: Ch 1, hdc in first 4 hdc, change to E, hdc in next 9 hdc, change to D, hdc in next 3 hdc, change to E, hdc in next hdc, change to B, hdc in next 2 hdc, change to E, hdc in next hdc, change to D, hdc in next 3 hdc, change to E, hdc in next 8 hdc, late change to A, hdc across, turn—4 A, 9 E, 3 D, 1 E, 2 B, 1 E, 3 D, 9 E, 4 A.

ROW 17: Ch 1, hdc in first 4 hdc, change to E, hdc in next 3 hdc, change to A, hdc in next 4 hdc, change to E, hdc in next 2 hdc, change to D, hdc in next 3 hdc, change to E, hdc in next 4 hdc, change to D, hdc in next 3 hdc, change to E, hdc in next 2 hdc, change to A, hdc in next 4 hdc, late change to E, hdc in next 3 hdc, late change to A, hdc across, turn—4 A, 3 E, 4 A, 2 E, 3 D, 4 E, 3 D, 2 E, 5 A, 3 E, 3 A.

ROW 18: Ch 1, hdc in first 3 hdc, change to E, hdc in next 3 hdc, change to A, hdc in next 5 hdc, change to E, hdc in next 14 hdc, change to A, hdc in next 4 hdc, late change to E, hdc in next 3 hdc, late change to A, hdc across, turn—3 A, 3 E, 5 A, 14 E, 5 A, 3 E, 3 A.

ROW 19: Ch 1, hdc in first 3 hdc, late change to E, hdc in next 3 hdc, change to A, hdc in next 5 hdc, change to E, hdc in next 14 hdc, change to A, hdc in next 5 hdc, late change to E, hdc in next 3 hdc, change to A, hdc across, turn—4 A, 2 E, 5 A, 14 E, 6 A, 2 E, 3 A.

ROW 20: Ch 1, hdc in first 3 hdc, change to E, hdc in next 2 hdc, late change to A, hdc in next 9 hdc, hdc-sc-tog, change to E, 2 hdc

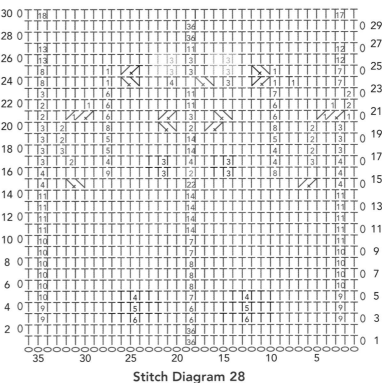

Stitch Diagram 28

in next hdc, hdc in next 2 hdc, 2 hdc in next hdc, late change to A, hdc-sc-tog, hdc in next 8 hdc, change to E, hdc in next 2 hdc, late change to A, hdc across, turn—3 A, 3 E, 9 A, 7 E, 8 A, 3 E, 3 A.

ROW 21: Ch 1, hdc in first hdc, hdc-sc-tog, change to E, hdc in next hdc, change to A, 2 hdc in next hdc, late change to E, hdc in next hdc, late change to A, hdc in next 7 hdc, 2 hdc in next hdc, change to E, hdc-sc-tog, hdc in next 3 hdc, hdc-sc-tog, change to A, 2 hdc in next hdc, hdc in next 6 hdc, hdc-sc-tog, change to E, hdc in next hdc, change to A, 2 hdc in next hdc, late change to E, hdc in next hdc, late change to A, hdc across, turn—2 A, 1 E, 3 A, 1 E, 8 A, 5 E, 9 A, 1 E, 3 A, 1 E, 2 A.

ROW 22: Ch 1, hdc in first 2 hdc, late change to E, hdc in next hdc, late change to A, hdc in next 3 hdc, change to E, hdc in next hdc, change to A, hdc in next 6 hdc, change to E, hdc in next 11 hdc, change to A, hdc in next 5 hdc, late change to E, hdc in next hdc, late change to A, hdc in next 3 hdc, change to E, hdc in next hdc, change to A, hdc across, turn—3 A, 1 E, 2 A, 1 E, 6 A, 11 E, 6 A, 1 E, 2 A, 1 E, 2 A.

ROW 23: Ch 1, hdc in first 2 hdc, late change to E, hdc in next hdc, change to A, hdc in next 2 hdc, late change to E, hdc in next hdc, change to A, hdc in next 6 hdc, change to E, hdc in next 11 hdc, change to A, hdc in next 6 hdc, late change to E, hdc in next hdc, change to A, hdc in next 2 hdc, late change to E, hdc in next hdc, change to A, hdc across, turn—12 A, 11 E, 13 A.

ROW 24: Ch 1, hdc in first 8 hdc, change to D, hdc in next hdc, change to A, hdc in next hdc, hdc-sc-tog, change to D, 2 hdc in next hdc, change to E, hdc in next 4 hdc, late change to B, hdc in next hdc, hdc-sc-tog, change to E, 2 hdc in next hdc, hdc in next 3 hdc, change to D, 2 hdc in next hdc, change to A, hdc-sc-tog, hdc in next hdc, change to D, hdc in next hdc, change to A, hdc across, turn—8 A, 1 D, 2 A, 2 D, 5 E, 1 B, 5 E, 2 D, 2 A, 1 D, 7 A.

ROW 25: Ch 1, hdc in first 7 hdc, late change to D, hdc in next hdc, change to A, hdc in next hdc, 2 hdc in next hdc, late change to D, hdc-sc-tog, change to E, hdc in next hdc, change to C, hdc in next 3 hdc, change to E, hdc in next 3 hdc, change to C, hdc in next 3 hdc, change to E, hdc in next hdc, change to D, hdc-sc-tog, change to A, 2 hdc in next hdc, hdc in next hdc, late change to D, hdc in next hdc, change to A, hdc across, turn—12 A, 1 E, 3 C, 3 E, 3 C, 1 E, 1 D, 12 A.

ROW 26: Ch 1, hdc in first 13 hdc, change to E, hdc in next hdc, change to C, hdc in next 3 hdc, change to E, hdc in next 3 hdc, change to C, hdc in next 3 hdc, change to E, hdc in next hdc, change to A, hdc across, turn—13 A, 1 E, 3 C, 3 E, 3 C, 1 E, 12 A.

ROW 27: Ch 1, hdc in first 12 hdc, change to E, hdc in next 11 hdc, change to A, hdc across, turn—12 A, 11 E, 13 A.

ROWS 28 AND 29: Ch 1, hdc in each hdc across, turn.

ROW 30: Ch 1, hdc in first 18 hdc, late change to D, hdc in next hdc, change to A, hdc across—36 A. Fasten off and weave in ends.

CHAPTER 4
Afghans

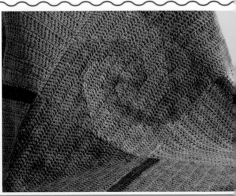

Learn Reversible Intarsia Sampler

The nine squares in this sampler afghan are designed to teach you all of the stitches used in the reversible intarsia technique. You begin with upright half double and double crochet stitches, then move through the various angles of half double crochet, and finally use half-color double crochet stitches. Once you master the technique with these nine squares, you will have learned the skills to be able to complete any of the patterns in this book. The squares featured here also ease you into colorwork, beginning with two colors and gradually working up to as many as five to seven separate bobbins of color within a single square.

Yarn

Worsted weight (#4 Medium). Shown Here: Berocco, Comfort (50% super fine nylon, 50% super fine acrylic; 210 yd [193 m]/3.5 oz [100 g]): 2 skeins each Duck Teal #9759 (A), Raspberry Coulis #9717 (B), Seedling #9740 (light green; C), and Spanish Brown #9727 (D); 4 skeins Dried Plum #9780 (E).

Hook

H/8 (5.0 mm) or hook needed to obtain gauge.

Notions

Size 16 tapestry or yarn needle; scissors.

Gauge

14 hdc × 12 rows = 4" × 4" (10 × 10 cm). 14 dc × 9 rows = 4" × 4" (10 × 10 cm).

Finished Size

Each square measures about 10½" × 10½" (26.5 × 26.5 cm), including 2 rounds of single crochet edging. With a 3½" (9 cm) border, finished blanket measures about 37" × 37" (94 × 94 cm).

Notes

- The WS of the square is the back side of your sc edging. Although all the squares are reversible, it is helpful to be clear about which is the wrong side for consistency when joining squares.

- When crocheting into the side stitches on edges, always insert the hook under 2 strands of yarn.

- "Sashing" is a term used in quilting for strips of fabric sewn between quilt blocks. The squares in this sampler are joined by alternating double crochets worked in the edges of one square and then the other, to create a no-sew "sashing" between the squares.

- The method used for joining the squares may appear to create too many stitches to lie flat. However, once the squares are pulled apart, the stitches will gather together to create just a slightly raised "seam" on one side. The gathered stitches appear more decorative than a traditional single crochet or slip-stitched seam.

- Refer to the layout diagram on page 93 for assistance.

Pattern

Make 1 of each of the following squares according to the instructions in Chapter 2: 1, 2, 3, 5, 6, 7, 9, 10, and 11.

SQUARE FINISHING AND ARRANGEMENT

Work 2 rows sc edging around each square as described on page 16. Arrange squares as shown in the layout diagram at right or as desired.

Joining Squares and Strips

Join the squares into vertical strips or columns as described below, then join strips in the same manner.

Sashing Between Squares to Form Strips 1–3:
With WS facing up, lay 2 squares out next to each other. Join color E with sl st in corner st of first square, ch 2, dc in corner st of second square. Working back and forth between the 2 squares, alternate working 1 dc in each sc across, first square, then second square, until you have reached the opposite corner sts on both squares. Finish off. Repeat with second and third squares, to form 1 strip.

Sashing Between Strips:
With WS facing up, lay Strips 1 and 2 out next to each other. Join color E with sl st in top corner st of first strip, ch 2, dc in corner st of second strip. Working back and forth between the 2 strips, alternate working 1 dc in each sc across to corner sts on first squares, [continue alternating between Strips 1 and 2 and work 5 dc evenly across side sts of sashing between squares, alternate working 1 dc in each sc across to corner sts on next 2 squares] 2 times. Finish off. Repeat with Strips 2 and 3.

Border

With WS facing, join with sl st in third sc of any corner.

RND 1: Ch 1, sc in same sc and each sc across edging of first square, [work 5 sc evenly across side sts of sashing between squares, sc in each sc across edging of next square] 2 times, *3 sc in second sc at corner, sc in each sc across edging of first square, [work 5 sc evenly across side sts of sashing between squares, sc in each sc across edging of next square] 2 times, repeat from * 2 more times, 2 sc in same sc as first sc, join with sl st in first sc—524 sc.

RND 2: Ch 1, dc in same sc and each sc across to second sc at corner, [(dc, ch 1, dc) in second sc at corner, dc in each sc across to next corner] 3 times, [dc, ch 1, dc] in second sc at corner, join with sl st in first dc—528 dc.

RNDS 3–7: Ch 1, [dc in same dc and each dc across to ch-1 sp at corner, (dc, ch 1, dc) in ch-1 sp] 4 times, dc in any remaining dc, join with sl st in first dc—568 dc.

RND 8: Ch 1, [sc in each dc across to ch-1 sp, (sc, ch 1, sc) in ch-1 sp] 4 times, sc in any remaining dc, join with sl st in first sc—572 sc.

RND 9: Ch 1, working back in the other direction, rev sc in last sc of previous rnd and each sc around, skipping ch-1 sps, join with sl st in beg ch-1. Fasten off.

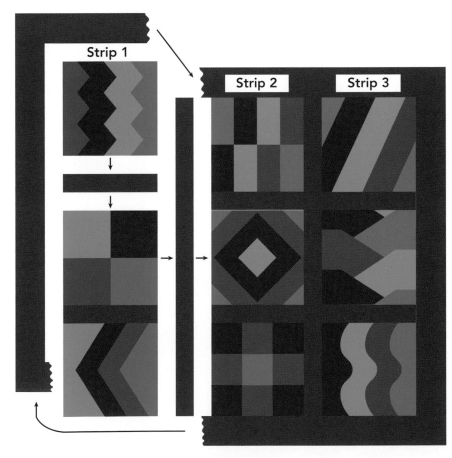

Layout Diagram

Grandpa Kit's Garden

I first learned about intarsia from my father's knitting, so it seemed only fitting to name this afghan after him. My father is quite the Renaissance man. In addition to knitting, playing the harp, and raising rare breeds of tropical fish, he is an avid gardener. He has shared that passion with my children through regular afternoons spent in his garden, planting seeds and watching them grow. They help him harvest fruits and vegetables, most of which he donates to local food pantries. And then of course, there are the flowers. . . .

Yarn

Worsted weight (#4 Medium). **Shown Here:** Red Heart, With Love (100% acrylic; 390 yd [357 m]/7 oz [198 g]): 5 skeins #1805 Bluebell (A); 2 skeins #1620 Clover (B); 1 skein each #1538 Lilac (C), #1207 Cornsilk (D), and #1321 Chocolate (E).

Hook

J/10 (6.0 mm) or hook needed to obtain gauge.

Notions

Size 16 tapestry or large yarn needle; scissors; stitch markers.

Gauge

14 hdc × 12 rows = 4" × 4" (10 × 10 cm).

Finished Size

Each square measures about 12" × 12" (30.5 × 30.5 cm). With a 2" (5 cm) border,

finished blanket measures about 52" × 64" (132 × 162.5 cm).

Notes

- Make sure the beginning chain of each square is not too loose, or gaps will show when they are whipstitched together.

- Solid squares may come out slightly larger than the colorwork squares, but will balance each other out when they are sewn together.

- Four of the leaf squares and all of the solid squares will be WS up when sewn together to create a consistent pattern in the rows of stitches.

- Leave long tails for sewing (about 2½ yd [2.3 m]), when beginning and ending each square.

- To create smoother seams, when whipstitching strips together, work through only 1 loop of sides of stitches (being careful to match the rows).

- When crocheting into the side stitches on edges, always insert hook under 2 strands of yarn.

- On first round of the border, work 36 stitches across sides of each square. Use stitch markers to mark the center and beginning of squares to help evenly distribute stitches down sides.

- For the Small and Large Grass Stitch on the last round of the border, work into the back bump of the chains rather than front or back loops.

- Refer to the layout diagram on page 97 for assistance.

Pattern

Complete the following squares: 2 each of #17 Tulip and #18 Daisy; 6 of #19 Stem with Leaf; 4 of #20 Stem with Grass; 1 of #21 Dragonfly; 1 of #22 Sun.

SOLID SQUARES (MAKE 4)

With A, ch 37.

ROW 1: Hdc in second ch from hook and each ch across, turn—36 hdc.

ROWS 2–30: Ch 1, hdc in each hdc across, turn. Finish off.

JOINING SQUARES

Arrange the squares as shown in the layout diagram at right, noting which squares should be RS or WS up. Join the squares into 4 vertical strips or columns by whipstitching the top row of one square to the unused loops of the beginning chain of the square above it, inserting the needle under both loops of the stitch and unused chain. Then whipstitch the strips together, inserting the needle under just one loop of side stitches of rows. Be careful to match the rows in each square, and always work in the same direction for consistency of stitches.

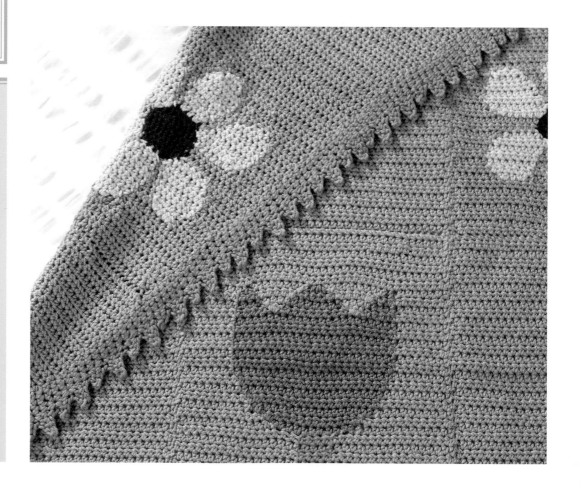

BORDER

With RS facing, join B with sl st in upper corner st (to prepare for working down the long side of the afghan in the following rnds).

RND 1: Ch 1, sc in same st, *work 178 sc evenly down side, 3 sc in top of corner st*, 142 sc across rem unused lps of beg ch to corner, 3 sc in last st at corner, rep from * to *, 142 sc in each st across tops of strips, 2 sc in first sc used, join with sl st in first dc. Do not turn—652 sc.

RND 2: Ch 1, [sc in each sc across to corner, 3 sc in second sc of corner] 4 times, join with sl st to first sc—660 sc.

RND 3: Ch 1, [sc in each sc across to corner, 3 sc in second sc of corner] 4 times, do not join—668 sc.

RND 4: Lg-gr, sk 2 sc, *[sm-gr, sk 1 sc, lg-gr, sk 2 sc] rep across to last 5 sc before corner, sm-gr, lg-gr, sk 1 sc, sm-gr, lg-gr, rep from * 3 more times, join with sl st in same sc as first sl st—612 sl st.

Fasten off.

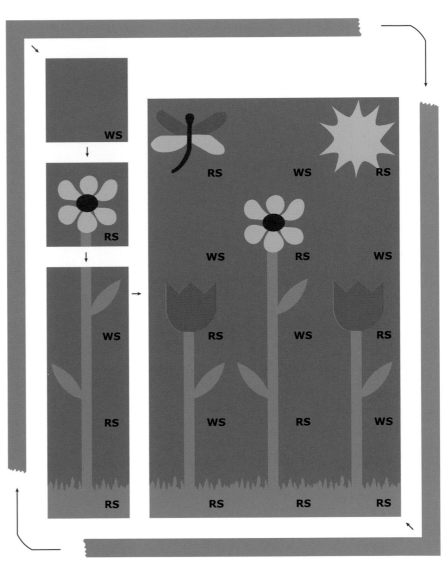

Layout Diagram

Jen and Ivo's Wedding Quilt

I began working on this afghan while traveling to the wedding of two dear friends. Being someone who is unable to sit still without yarn and hook in my hands, I started the log cabin square as I waited for the ceremony to begin. When the bride began walking down the aisle, I saw that she was wearing a dress in a beautiful shade of green, along with a peacock-blue crocheted shrug. The colors of her ensemble matched those featured in the square I was crocheting at that very moment! I knew immediately that this afghan was meant for the happy couple.

Yarn

Worsted weight (#4 Medium).

Shown Here: Plymouth Yarn, Encore (75% acrylic, 25% wool; 200 yd [183 m]/3.5 oz [100 g]): 1 skein each #0045 English Fern, #0801 Colonial Green, and #0555 Briston Wedgewood (dark blue); 2 skeins #0469 Storm Blue; 5 skeins #0462 Woodbine (dark green).

Please Note: Yarn colors are not assigned letter designations here because they will be assigned differing letters for each of the squares. See the pattern for further information.

Hook

G/6 (4.0 mm) or hook needed to obtain gauge.

Notions

Size 16 tapestry or yarn needle; scissors.

Gauge

14 hdc × 12 rows = 4" × 4" (10 × 10 cm). 14 dc × 9 rows = 4" × 4" (10 × 10 cm).

Finished Size

Each square measures about 11" × 11" (28 × 28 cm), including 2 rounds of single crochet edging. Finished blanket measures about 44½" × 44½" (113 × 113 cm).

Notes

- When crocheting into the side stitches on edges, always insert the hook under 2 strands of yarn.

- The WS of the square is the back side of your sc edging. Although all the squares are reversible, it is helpful to be clear about which is the wrong side for consistency when joining squares.

- "Sashing" is a term used in quilting for strips of fabric sewn between quilt blocks. The squares in this sampler are joined by working double crochets back and forth between the squares, to create a no-sew "sashing" between the squares.

- Refer to the layout diagram on page 101 for assistance.

Pattern

Complete 1 of each of the squares listed as follows, using the indicated colors.

SQUARE 2
Color A: #0045 English Fern

Color B: #0801 Colonial Green

Color C: #0555 Briston Wedgewood

Color D: #0469 Storm Blue

SQUARES 4, 12, AND 14
Color A: #0469 Storm Blue

Color B: #0462 Woodbine

Color C: #0555 Briston Wedgewood

Color D: #0045 English Fern

Color E: #0801 Colonial Green

SQUARES 8, 9, 13, AND 15
Color A: #0469 Storm Blue

Color B: #0045 English Fern

Color C: #0801 Colonial Green

Color D: #0555 Briston Wedgewood

SQUARE 16
Color A: #0045 English Fern

Color B: #0469 Storm Blue

Color C: #0801 Colonial Green

Color D: #0555 Briston Wedgewood

SQUARE FINISHING AND ARRANGEMENT
Work 2 rows sc edging around each square as described on page 16. Arrange squares as shown in the layout diagram on page 101, or in a pattern that appeals to you.

JOINING SQUARES/STRIPS
Join the squares into vertical strips or columns as described below, then join strips in the same manner.

Sashing Between Squares to Form Strips 1–3
With RS facing up, lay 2 squares out next to each other. Join E (#0801 Colonial Green) with sl st in second sc at corner of first square. Ch 6, sl st in second sc at corner of second square, ch 1, sk 1 sc, sl st in next sc of second square, turn.

ROW 1: Dc in each ch across, sl st in next unused sc on first square, ch 1, sk 1 sc, sl st in next sc, turn.

ROW 2: Dc in each dc across, sl st in next unused sc on second square, ch 1, sk 1 sc, sl st in next sc, turn.

ROW 3: Dc in each dc across, sl st in next

unused sc on first square, ch 1, sk 1 sc, sl st in next sc, turn.

ROWS 4–26: Alternate Rows 2 and 3. Fasten off. Rep with second and third squares, to form Strip 1. Rep with remaining squares to form Strips 2 and 3.

Sashing Between Strips

With RS facing up, lay Strips 1 and 2 out next to each other. Join as described below.

ROWS 1–26: Rep Rows 1–26 for Sashing Between Squares. Change to A on sl st at end of last row. Fasten off E.

ROWS 27–31: Alternate Rows 2 and 3, working into dcs and unused lps of beg ch on Sashing Between Squares. Change to E on sl st at end of last row. Fasten off A.

ROWS 32–57: Alternate Rows 2 and 3. Change to A on sl st at end of last row. Fasten off E.

ROWS 58–88: Rep Rows 27–57. Do not change to A on last row. Fasten off.

BORDER
Sides (complete on both sides):

With RS facing, join E with dc in second sc of one corner.

ROW 1: Dc in each sc across and in 6 dc or unused lps of beg chs on Sashing Between Squares, turn—132 dc.

ROWS 2–5: Ch 1, dc in first dc and each dc across, turn. Do not turn at end of last row. Fasten off.

Top and Bottom:

With RS facing, join A with dc in side of last st of Side Border at top of afghan.

ROW 1: Work 8 dc evenly across sides of Side Border sts, change to E, dc in each sc across and in 6 dc or unused lps of beg chs on Sashing Between Squares, change to A, work 8 dc evenly across sides of Side Border sts, turn—8 A, 132 E, 8 A.

ROWS 2–5: Ch 1, dc in first 8 dc, change to E, dc in next 132 dc, change to A, dc in next 8 dc, turn—8 A, 132 E, 8 A. Do not turn at end of last row. Fasten off.

Rep Rows 1–5 at bottom.

EDGING
With RS facing, join E with sl st in first st of Row 5 of Top Border.

RND 1: Ch 1, sc in each dc across to last dc, 3 sc in last dc (corner made), turn to work next side, work 7 dc evenly across sides of Top Border sts, sc in next 132 dc, work 7 dc evenly across sides of Bottom Border sts, 3 sc in top of last dc, turn to work next side, sc in next 146 dc, 3 sc in top of last dc, turn to work next side, work 7 dc evenly across sides of Bottom Border sts, sc in next 132 dc, work 7 dc evenly across sides of Top Border sts, 2 sc in first dc at corner, join with sl st to first sc. Do not turn—596 sc.

RND 2: Ch 1, [sc in each sc across to corner, 3 sc in second sc of corner] 4 times, join with sl st to first sc—604 sc.

RND 3: Ch 1, [sc in each sc across to corner, 3 sc in second sc of corner] 4 times, sc in next sc, join with sl st to first sc—612 sc.

RND 4: Sl st loosely in each sc around, join with sl st through center of first sl st—612 sl st. Fasten off.

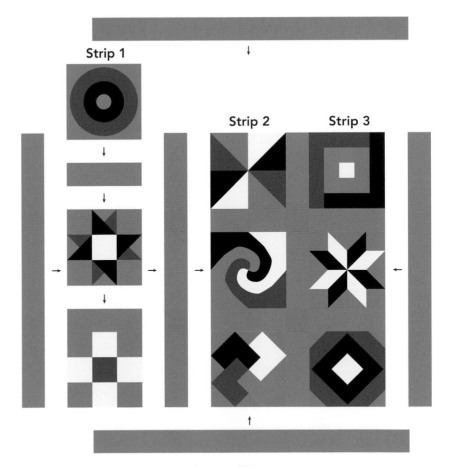

Layout Diagram

Tyler's Space Adventure

As I was busy developing ideas for this book, I got the idea to make a "community afghan" for a five-year-old boy named Tyler who was undergoing surgery. I enlisted the help of six friends who each made a solid-colored square in his favorite color to alternate with the picture squares I was making. We used a bulky-weight yarn so the squares worked up quickly and were large enough to make a cuddly afghan to cover his bed. We knew Tyler liked robots and squid, so with the help of my own son, we designed this space-themed afghan, which any young space enthusiast would be thrilled to receive.

Yarn
Worsted weight (#4 Medium).

Shown Here: Cascade, Pacific Chunky (60% acrylic, 40% superwash Merino wool; 120 yd [110 m]/3.5 oz [100 g]): 5 skeins #70 Classic Blue (A); 1 skein each #33 Cactus (B), #02 White (C), #53 Beet (D), #24 Platinum (E), and #48 Black (F); 7 skeins each #44 Italian Plum (G) and #610 Bluebird (H).

Hook
J/10 (6.0 mm) or hook needed to obtain gauge.

Notions
Large tapestry or yarn needle; scissors.

Gauge
11 hdc × 10 rows = 4" × 4" (10 × 10 cm).

Finished Size
Each square measures about 14½" × 14½" (37 × 37 cm), including 2 rounds of single crochet edging. With a 3" (7.5 cm) border, finished blanket measures about 50" × 64" (127 × 162.5 cm).

Notes
- The WS of the square is the back side of the sc edging. Although all the squares are reversible, it is helpful to be clear about which is the WS for consistency when joining squares.
- When working back into the tops of late color changes (late change to),

insert the hook under the carried yarn and front loop only, to avoid larger holes that can be left when working in chunky- or bulky-weight yarns.

- Solid squares may come out slightly larger than the colorwork squares, but will balance out when the same number of sc stitches are worked around each square before they are sewn together.

- When crocheting into the side stitches on edges, always insert the hook under 2 strands of yarn.

- Refer to the layout diagram on page 105 for assistance.

Puff Stitch (Puff st)

(Yo, insert hook into indicated st, yo, pull up loop out of st, pointing hook up to create a long loop) 4 times in same st, yo, pull through all 9 loops on hook, ch1.

Pattern

Complete 1 each of the 6 space-themed squares beginning on page 76, using colors A–H as indicated in this pattern.

SOLID SQUARES (MAKE 6)

With H, ch 37.

ROW 1: Hdc in second ch from hook and each ch across, turn—36 hdc.

ROWS 2–30: Ch 1, hdc in each hdc across, turn. Fasten off.

FINISHING

Work 2 rows sc edging around each square as described on page 16. Arrange squares as shown in the layout diagram or as desired.

Joining Squares

With RS together, join squares with sl st, matching each sc of second rnd of edging. First, work all horizontal seams to join squares, adding a diagonal sl st in each direction at the corners between squares.

Then work all vertical seams, skipping over the horizontal seam and continuing on to the next square. Use an iron to steam-press the seams flat from the back and then from the front.

Border

With RS facing, join E with sl st in last st at upper corner.

RND 1: Ch 1, sc in same sc, [sc in each sc across to second sc at corner, 3 sc in second sc] 3 times, sc in each sc across to first sc used, 2 sc in first sc used, join with sl st to first sc. Do not turn—564 sc.

RND 2: Ch 1, [dc in next 3 sc, Puff st in next sc, *dc in next 7 sc, Puff st in next sc* rep from * to * across to last 5 sc at corner, dc in next 4 sc, 5 dc in next sc] 4 times, join with sl st to first sc—580 sts.

RND 3: Ch 1, [sc in each dc and Puff st across to corner, skipping ch-1 sp after Puffs, 3 sc in second sc at corner] 4 times, sc in rem sts, join with sl st to first sc—588 sc.

RND 4: Ch 1, [sc in each sc across to corner, 3 sc in second sc at corner] 4 times, sc in rem sts, join with sl st to first sc—596 sc.

RND 5: Ch 1, [*Puff st in next sc, dc in next 7 sc*, rep from * to * across to last 4 sc at corner, dc in next 3 sc, 5 dc in next sc, dc in next 4 sc] 4 times, join with sl st to first sc—612 sts.

RNDS 6 AND 7: Rep Rnds 3 and 4—628 sts after Rnd 7.

RND 8: [Sl st in blo in each sc across to corner, sl st in blo of second sc at corner, ch 1] 4 times, sl st in next 8 sc, join with sl st through center of first sl st—628 sl st. Fasten off.

Layout Diagram

Outrageous Fortune

This was the first of several quilt-inspired afghans in this book that I decided to name after a quote from a Shakespearean play. Every time I thought of the Arrow and Bulls-eye squares, the quote from *Hamlet*, "...the slings and arrows of outrageous fortune..." came to mind. See if you can identify which Shakespearean play each of the other quilt names come from and how they are related to the quilts themselves.

Yarn
Worsted weight (#4 Medium).

Shown Here: Lion Brand, Vanna's Choice (100% acrylic; 210 yd [193 m]/3.5 oz [100 g]): 5 skeins #107 Sapphire (A), 6 skeins #173 Dusty Green (B), 5 skeins #134 Terracotta (pumpkin orange; C), and 5 skeins #180 Cranberry (D).

Hook
I/9 (5.5 mm) or hook needed to obtain gauge.

Notions
Size 16 tapestry or yarn needle; scissors; stitch markers.

Gauge
13 dc × 7 rows = 4" × 4" (10 × 10 cm).

Finished Size
Each square measures about 11½" × 11½" (29 × 29 cm). With a 2" (5 cm) border, finished blanket measures about 60" × 75" (152.5 × 190.5 cm).

Notes
- When crocheting into the side stitches on edges, always insert the hook under 2 strands of yarn.

- Leave long tails for sewing (about 2½ yd [2.3 m]) when beginning and ending each strip.

- To create smoother seams, when whipstitching strips together, be careful to match rows and work through only 1 strand of yarn on sides of stitches.

- On the first round of the border, work 36 stitches across sides of each square. Use stitch markers to mark the center and beginning of squares to help evenly distribute stitches down the sides.

- Refer to layout diagram on page 109 for assistance.

Pattern

STRIP 1 (MAKE 4)

Complete 6 Arrows (Square #11) worked continuously. Leave long tails of yarn for sewing at the beginning and end of each strip.

STRIP 2 (MAKE 1)

Complete 6 Bulls-eyes (Square #12) worked continuously. Use the yarn left from making 4 of Strip 1 for the rows where you need 2 balls of the same color.

FINISHING

Weave in all ends on Strip 2.

Joining Squares/Strips

Using the long ends left at the beginning and ending of each strip, whipstitch the strips together as shown in the layout diagram, noting which strips should be RS or WS up. Insert the needle under 1 strand of the side sts, being careful to match each st and row.

Border

Join Color B in upper corner of last row of last strip with sl st.

RND 1: Ch 1, sc in same st, *work 214 sc evenly down side, 3 sc in top of corner st*, 178 sc across rem unused lps of beg ch to corner, 3 sc in last st at corner, rep from * to *, 178 sc in each st across tops of strips, 2 sc in first sc used, join with sl st in first dc. Do not turn—796 sc.

RND 2: Ch 1, hdc in first st, [hdc in each st across to corner, 4 hdc in second st at corner] rep around, hdc in any rem sts, join with sl st in first hdc—808 hdc.

RND 3: Ch 1, hdc in first hdc, [hdc in each hdc across to corner, 3 hdc in third hdc at corner] rep around, hdc in rem hdcs, join with sl st in first hdc—816 hdc.

RNDS 4 AND 5: Rep Rnds 2 and 3—836 hdc after Rnd 5.

RND 6: Ch 1, [sc in each hdc across to corner, (sc, ch 1, sc) in second hdc at corner] 4 times, sc in rem hdc, join with sl st in first sc—840 sc.

Rnd 7: [Sl st in each sc across to next ch-1 sp, ch 1] 4 times, sl st in rem sc across, join with sl st in center of first sl st—840 sl st. Fasten off and weave in all ends.

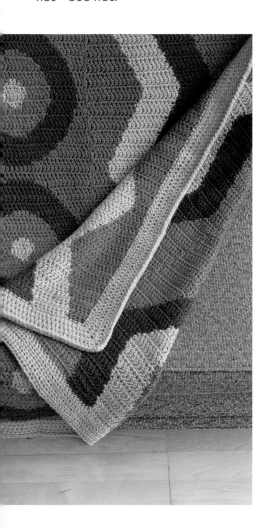

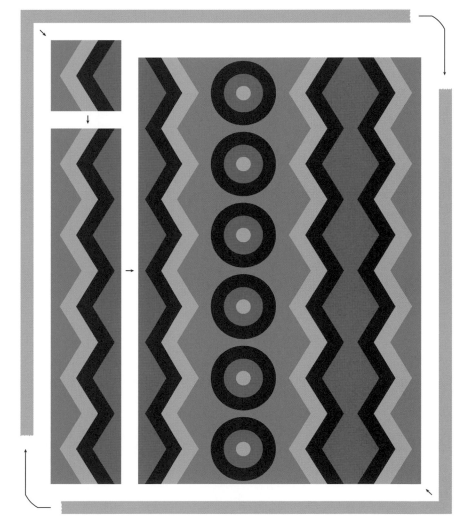

Layout Diagram

Shines So Bright

The sun and the moon are a common theme for decorating a baby's or child's bedroom. What better gift to celebrate the arrival of a new baby than a celestial-themed blanket (made in a bulky-weight yarn so you can whip it up quickly)? For this design, I wanted a layout that used just four picture squares, with a textured stitch in between them, and very little seaming. Although many of the afghans in this book actually require sewn seams to get a "seamless" effect, I love patterns that can be joined as you go, or crocheted together, rather than sewn.

Yarn
Chunky weight (#5 Bulky).

Shown Here: Lion Brand, Baby's 1st (55% acrylic, 45% cotton; 120 yd [110 m]/3.5 oz [100 g]): 9 skeins #925-146 Sea Sprite (A); 3 skeins Honey Bee #925-157 (B).

Hook
K/10.5 (6.5 mm) or hook needed to obtain gauge.

Notions
Large tapestry or yarn needle; scissors; stitch markers.

Gauge
10 hdc × 8 rows = 4" × 4" (10 × 10 cm).

Finished Size
Each square measures about 14½" × 14½" (37 × 37 cm). With a 1½" (3.8 cm) border, finished blanket measures about 40" × 48" (101.5 × 122 cm).

Notes
- Make sure the beginning chain of each square is not too loose, or gaps will show when they are whipstitched together.

- When working back into the tops of late color changes (late change to), insert the hook under the carried yarn and front loop only, to avoid larger holes that can be left when working with chunky- or bulky-weight yarns.

- Leave long tails for sewing (about 24" [61 cm]) when beginning each square.

- The Woven Stitch (see Glossary) is used to join the last 2 squares to create a smoother join in the bulky-weight yarn. When crocheting into the side stitches on edges, always insert the hook under 2 strands of yarn.

- On the first round of the border, work 36 stitches across the sides of each square and between squares. Use stitch markers to mark the center and beginning of squares to help evenly distribute stitches down sides.

- Refer to the layout diagram on page 113 for assistance.

Tip for Joining

When working back
and forth between 2
squares, it may seem
awkward to turn the
whole work over for
each row. Instead,
turn only the area
you are working and
bring just the yarn all
the way around to the
back of your work.

Alternative Design Idea

Choose any 2 of
your favorite picture
or quilt squares to
replace the Suns and
Moons in this layout.
Try Tulips and Daisies
without a stem or
any 2 of the space-
themed squares for a
completely different
theme.

Pattern

Complete 2 Sun (Square #22) and 2 Moon
(Square #23) squares, using color A as indicated in this pattern; use #925-157 Honey
Bee for color E in the Sun squares and for
color D in the Moon squares.

JOINING FIRST TWO SQUARES

With RS facing up, lay 1 Moon and 1 Sun square
out next to each other. Join color A with sl st in
corner of Moon square. Ch 21, sl st in corner of
Sun square and side st of row 1, turn.

ROW 1: Sc in each ch across, sl st in side of
Row 2 of Moon square, ch 1, sk 1 row on Moon
square, sl st in side of next row, turn—21 sc.

ROW 2: 3 dc in first sc (counts as first shell),
[sk 3 sc, shell in next sc] 4 times, sk 3 sc, sc in
last sc, sl st in side of next row of Sun square,
ch 1, sk 1 row of Sun square, sl st in side of
next row, turn—5 shells.

ROWS 3–19: 3 dc in first sc, [sk 3 dc, shell in
next ch-2 sp] 4 times, sk 3 dc, sc in sp between
3 dc and turning sl st, sl st in side of next row
of opposite square, ch 1, sk 1 row, sl st in side
of next row, turn—5 shells. Finish off.

ROW 20: 3 dc in first sc, [sk 3 dc, shell in next
ch-2 sp] 4 times, sk 3 dc, sc in sp between 3
dc and turning sl st, sl st in side of next row
of opposite square—5 shells. Fasten off. Turn
work, WS facing.

CENTER OF AFGHAN

ROW 1: Join A with sl st in first st of top row of
Sun square, ch 3, 3 dc in same st (counts as first
shell), *[sk 3 sc, shell in next sc] 8 times*, shell
in same sp as last sl st of Row 20, [sk 3 dc, shell
in next ch-2 sp] 4 times, shell in sp between
next 3 dc and turning sl st, rep from * to *, sc in
last st of Moon square, turn—23 shells.

ROWS 2–19: Ch 3, 3 dc in first sc, [sk 3 dc, shell
in next ch-2 sp] rep across to turning ch, sc in
ch-3 sp, turn—23 shells.

ROW 20: Ch 1, dc in first sc, hdc in next 2 dc,
*[sc in next dc, sk ch-2 sp, dc in first sc, hdc in
next 2 dc]* 8 times, shell in next ch-2 sp, [sk
3 dc, shell in next ch-2 sp] 4 times, sk next
sc and 2 dc, rep from * to * 9 times, sc in last
dc. Fasten off, leaving a long tail (about 24"
[61 cm]) for sewing on next square.

JOINING LAST TWO SQUARES

With RS facing, match the unused beg ch lps
of the remaining squares with the top sts
of Row 20 of Center. Use Woven Stitch (see
Glossary on page 141) to attach the remaining Sun and Moon squares to the flat portions
of Row 20, as shown in diagram. With WS
facing, join A with sl st in inside edge st of
second row of Moon square.

ROW 1: 3 dc in first sc, [sk 3 dc, shell in next ch-2 sp] 4 times, sk 3 dc, sc in next ch-2 sp, sl st in side st of second row of Sun square, ch 1, sk 1 row, sl st in side of next row, turn—5 shells.

ROWS 2–19: 3 dc in first sc, [sk 3 dc, shell in next ch-2 sp] 4 times, sk 3 dc, sc in space between 3 dc and turning sl st, sl st in side of next row of opposite square, ch 1, sk 1 row, sl st in side of next row, turn—5 shells.

ROW 20: Ch 1, dc in first sc, hdc in next 2 dc, [sc in next dc, skip ch-2 sp, dc in first sc, hdc in next 2 dc] 4 times, sc in last dc.

ROW 21: Sc in each ch across, sl st in side of Row 2 of Moon square, ch 1, sk 1 row, sl st in side of next row, turn—21sc. Fasten off.

BORDER

With RS facing, join A with sl st in corner of upper Moon square.

RND 1: Ch 1, sc in same st, *work 106 sc evenly across side to corner st, 3 sc in corner st*, work 91 sc in unused beg ch lps, 3 sc in corner st, rep from * to *, work 91 sc in each st across top, 2 sc in same sc as first sc, join with sl st in first sc—406 sc.

RND 2: Ch 1, sc in same sc, [sc in each sc across to second sc at corner, 3 sc in second sc at corner] 4 times, join with sl st in first sc. Fasten off—414 sc.

RND 3: Join B with sl st in first sc of Rnd 2, rep Rnd 2. Fasten off—422 sc.

RND 4: Sl st in next 2 sc, ch 1, [edge-sh in next sc, sk 2 sc] across to second sc at corner, edge-sh in next sc, sk 1 sc] 4 times, edge-sh in last sc, join with sl st in first sc. Fasten off—142 shells.

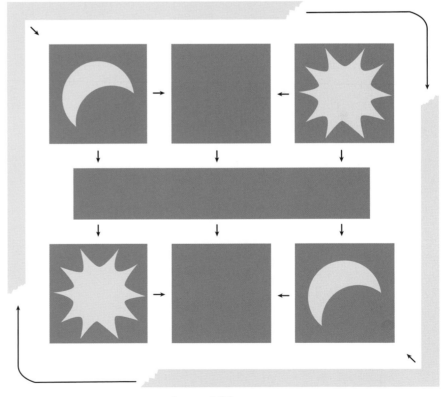

Layout Diagram

A World Too Wide

The square repeated throughout this afghan was orginally designed differently than what you see here, but a quilter-friend of mine commented that it looked similar to the traditional Snail's Trail or Drunkard's Path quilt-block patterns. With a few minor changes, I was able to create the distinctive spirals of the Snail's Trail using reversible double crochet stitches. The success of following that quilt inspiration led me to other quilt-inspired squares, opening up a whole world of afghan possibilities.

Yarn

DK weight (#3 Light).

Shown Here: Brown Sheep, Cotton Fleece (80% cotton, 20% Merino wool; 215 yd [197 m]/3.5 oz [100 g]):

2 skeins each:

Color 1: CW-860 Sedona Red

Color 2: CW-120 Honey Butter

Color 3: CW-455 Willow Leaf

Color 4: CW-825 Truffle

Color 6: CW-822 Milk Chocolate Chip

Color 7: CW-400 New Age Teal

Color 8: CW-105 Putty

Color 10: CW-780 Hearty Merlot

1 skein:

Color 5: CW-310 Wild Orange

3 skeins:

Color 9: CW-625 Terracotta Canyon

Please Note: Colors are identified by number in this pattern because different color combinations will be used for A, B, C, and D in the same square pattern.

Hook

G/6 (4.0 mm) or hook needed to obtain gauge.

Notions

Size 16 tapestry or yarn needle; scissors; stitch markers.

Gauge

14 dc × 9 rows = 4" × 4" (10 × 10 cm).

Finished Size

Each square measures about 10" × 10" (25.5 × 25.5 cm). With a 3" (7.5 cm) border, finished blanket measures about 56" × 66" (142 × 168 cm).

Notes

- When making Strips, colors A and B will always be the same as colors C and D

from the previous square, so the squares can be worked continuously rather than changing colors at the beginning of each square.

- When crocheting into the side stitches on edges, always insert the hook under 2 strands of yarn from side of stitch.

- To create smoother stitches, whipstitch strips together, working through 1 strand when joining sides of stitches.

- On the first round of the border, work 36 stitches across sides of each square. Use stitch markers to mark center and beginning of squares to help evenly distribute stitches down sides.

- Refer to the layout diagram on page 117.

Pattern

Complete 5 strips, each composed of 6 Snail's Trails (Square #16) worked continuously as follows. Leave long tails, about 18" (45.5 cm) long, for sewing at the beginning of each strip and when a new color is joined at the beg of Row 12 on each square.

STRIP 1

SQUARE 1: (A) Color 1, (B) Color 2, (C) Color 3, (D) Color 4

SQUARE 2: (A) Color 3, (B) Color 4, (C) Color 5, (D) Color 6

SQUARE 3: (A) Color 5, (B) Color 6, (C) Color 2, (D) Color 7

SQUARE 4: (A) Color 2, (B) Color 7, (C) Color 4, (D) Color 8

SQUARE 5: (A) Color 4, (B) Color 8, (C) Color 9, (D) Color 3

SQUARE 6: (A) Color 9, (B) Color 3, (C) Color 6, (D) Color 7

STRIP 2

SQUARE 1: (A) Color 7, (B) Color 1, (C) Color 8, (D) Color 3

SQUARE 2: (A) Color 8, (B) Color 3, (C) Color 1, (D) Color 5

SQUARE 3: (A) Color 1, (B) Color 5, (C) Color 6, (D) Color 2

SQUARE 4: (A) Color 6, (B) Color 2, (C) Color 3, (D) Color 4

SQUARE 5: (A) Color 3, (B) Color 4, (C) Color 2, (D) Color 9

SQUARE 6: (A) Color 2, (B) Color 9, (C) Color 5, (D) Color 6

STRIP 3

SQUARE 1: (A) Color 6, (B) Color 7, (C) Color 2, (D) Color 8

SQUARE 2: (A) Color 2, (B) Color 8, (C) Color 4, (D) Color 1

SQUARE 3: (A) Color 4, (B) Color 1, (C) Color 8, (D) Color 6

SQUARE 4: (A) Color 8, (B) Color 6, (C) Color 7, (D) Color 3

SQUARE 5: (A) Color 7, (B) Color 3, (C) Color 1, (D) Color 2

SQUARE 6: (A) Color 1, (B) Color 2, (C) Color 8, (D) Color 5

STRIP 4

SQUARE 1: (A) Color 9, (B) Color 6, (C) Color 7, (D) Color 2

SQUARE 2: (A) Color 7, (B) Color 2, (C) Color 3, (D) Color 4

SQUARE 3: (A) Color 3, (B) Color 4, (C) Color 1, (D) Color 8

SQUARE 4: (A) Color 1, (B) Color 8, (C) Color 6, (D) Color 7

SQUARE 5: (A) Color 6, (B) Color 7, (C) Color 4, (D) Color 1

SQUARE 6: (A) Color 4, (B) Color 1, (C) Color 2, (D) Color 8

STRIP 5

SQUARE 1: (A) Color 2, (B) Color 9, (C) Color 1, (D) Color 7

SQUARE 2: (A) Color 1, (B) Color 7, (C) Color 8, (D) Color 3

SQUARE 3: (A) Color 8, (B) Color 3, (C) Color 4, (D) Color 1

SQUARE 4: (A) Color 4, (B) Color 1, (C) Color 5, (D) Color 6

SQUARE 5: (A) Color 5, (B) Color 6, (C) Color 7, (D) Color 4

SQUARE 6: (A) Color 7, (B) Color 4, (C) Color 3, (D) Color 2

Layout Diagram

JOINING STRIPS AND FINISHING

Weave in all ends on each strip except long yarn tails for sewing (left at the beginning of new colors).

Joining Strips

Whipstitch the strips together as shown in the layout diagram, using the long tails already attached to the sides of each strip to match the colors of the squares. Insert the needle under 1 strand from the side sts, being careful to match each row. Before finishing off a color, run the yarn under the sts on either side of the join, to create a straighter line between the colors.

Border

Join Color 10 in upper corner of last row of Strip 5 with sl st.

RND 1: Ch 1, sc in same st, *work 214 sc evenly down side, 3 sc in top of corner st*, 178 sc across rem unused lps of beg ch to corner, 3 sc in last st at corner, rep from * to *, 178 sc in each st across tops of strips, 2 sc in first sc used, join with sl st in first dc—796 sc.

RND 2: Ch 1, dc in first sc, [dc in each sc across to corner, (2 dc, ch 1, 2 dc) in second sc at corner] rep around, dc in next sc, join with sl st in first dc. Finish off—808 dc.

RND 3: Join Color 9 with sc in first sc of prev rnd, *[dc in next dc, sc in next dc] across to last dc at corner, sk last dc, (sc, dc, sc, dc, sc) in ch-1 sp at corner, sk next dc, rep from * 3 more times, sc in next dc, join with sl st in first sc—816 sts.

RND 4: Ch 1, *[dc in next sc, sc in next dc] across to last sc at corner, (dc, sc, dc) in sc at corner, rep from * 3 more times, [sc in next dc, dc in next sc] across to last dc of prev rnd, sc in last dc, join with sl st in first dc—824 sts.

RND 5: Ch 1, *[sc in next dc, dc in next sc] across to last sc at corner, (dc, sc, dc) in sc at corner, rep from * 3 more times, [sc in next dc, dc in next sc] across to first sc, join with sl st in first sc—832 sts.

RNDS 6–9: Rep Rnds 4 and 5—864 sts after Rnd 9. Finish off.

RND 10: Join Color 10 with sl st in first dc, ch 1, [dc in each st across to corner, (2 dc, ch 1, 2 dc) in second sc at corner] rep around, dc in rem dc, join with sl st in first dc. Finish off—880 dc.

RND 11: Ch 1, [sc in each dc across to ch 1-sp, (sc, ch 1, sc) in ch-1 sp] 4 times, sc in rem dc, join with sl st in first sc—888 sc.

RND 12: [Sl st in each sc across to next ch-1 sp, ch 1] 4 times, sl st in rem sc across, join with sl st in center of first sl st—888 sl sts. Fasten off and weave in all ends.

Nine Lives

This blanket is dedicated to the memory of my three cats, Kidget, Jerry, and Cinnamon, whose long lives each came to an end as I was working on this book. We always knew having three cats so close in age meant they would all get old around the same time. I'm just glad I got to spend so much time sitting and crocheting blanket samples in their last few months, giving them company and a lap to sit on (when it wasn't full of yarn).

Yarn
Chunky weight (#5 Bulky).

Shown Here: Sweet Georgia, Superwash Chunky (100% superwash Merino wool; 120 yd [109 m]/3.5 oz [100 g]): 5 skeins each Riptide (deep blue) and Deep Olive (dark brown-green); 3 skeins Boysenberry (purple); 2 skeins Black Plum (deep red-purple).
Please Note: Yarn colors are not assigned letter designations here because they will be assigned differing letters for each of the squares. See the pattern for further information.

Hook
K/10½ (6.5 mm) or hook needed to obtain gauge.

Notions
Large yarn needle; scissors; stitch markers.

Gauge
9 dc × 6 rows = 4" × 4" (10 × 10 cm).

Finished Size
Each square measures about 15" × 15" (38 × 38 cm). With a 3" (7.5 cm) border, finished blanket measures about 51" × 51" (129.5 × 129.5 cm).

Notes
- Make sure the beginning chain of each square is not too loose, or gaps will show when they are whipstitched together.

- Solid squares may come out slightly larger than the colorwork squares, but should balance each other out when they are sewn together.

- When working back into the tops of late color changes (late change to), insert hook under carried yarn and front loop only, to avoid larger holes that can be left when working in chunky- or bulky-weight yarns.

- Leave long tails (about 24" [61 cm]) when beginning and ending each square (for sewing squares together).

- To create smoother seams, whipstitch squares together, working through 2 loops of top row of stitches or unused loops of beginning chains; work through only 1 strand of yarn when joining sides of stitches together.

- When crocheting into the side stitches on edges, always insert the hook under 2 strands of yarn.

- On the first round of the Border, work 36 stitches across sides of each square. Use stitch markers to mark center and beginning of squares to help evenly distribute stitches down sides.

- Refer to the layout diagram on page 123 for assistance.

Pattern

TAIL SQUARE

Make one Snail's Trail (Square #16) using Riptide as colors A and D and Deep Olive as colors B and C. Leave long tails for sewing squares together.

SOLID BODY SQUARES (MAKE 2 EACH WITH RIPTIDE AND DEEP OLIVE)

Ch 38.

ROW 1: Dc in third ch from hook and each ch across, turn—36 dc.

ROWS 2–22: Ch 1, dc in each dc across, turn.

Finish off, leaving long tail for sewing.

CAT-HEAD SQUARES

Make 2 each with Riptide and Deep Olive as color A. All heads will use Black Plum as color B and Boysenberry as color C.

With Black Plum (B), ch 38.

ROW 1: Dc in second ch from hook and each ch across, turn—36 dc.

ROW 2: Ch 1, dc in each dc across, turn. Finish off. Join A.

ROWS 3–15: Ch 1, dc in each dc across, turn.

ROW 16: Ch 1, dc in first 9 dc, dc2tog, change to C, 2 dc in next dc, dc in next 12 dc, 2 dc in next dc, change to A, dc-2tog, dc across, turn—10 A, 16 C, 10 A.

ROWS 17–21: Ch 1, dc in each dc to last 3 A-color dc, dc2tog, change to C, 2 dc in next dc, dc in each dc to last A-color dc, 2 dc in next dc, change to A, dc2tog, dc across, turn.

ROW 22: Ch 1, dc2tog, change to C, 2 dc in next dc, dc in next 30 dc, 2 dc in next dc, change to A, dc2tog, dc across, turn—10 A, 16 C, 10 A. Finish off, leaving long tail for sewing.

JOINING SQUARES/STRIPS

Weave in short ends on tail and head squares. Use long tails in same color as body squares of the cat you are joining to whipstitch squares together as follows: Join last row of body squares to beg ch of head squares to form 4 cats. Join sides of body squares to tail square as shown in the layout diagram. Join beg ch of body squares to sides of head squares.

BORDER

Join Boysenberry with sl st in any corner dc of assembled afghan.

RND 1: Ch 1, sc in same dc, work 71 sc evenly across side sts of cat head and body squares, sc in next 35 dc, [3 sc in last dc, work 71 sc evenly across side sts of cat head and body squares, sc in next 35 dc] 3 times, 2 sc in first dc used, join with sl st in first sc—436 sc.

RND 2: Ch 1, [dc in each sc across to second sc at corner, (2 dc, ch 1, 2 dc) in second sc at corner] 4 times, join with sl st in first dc—448 dc.

RND 3: Ch 1, [dc in each sc across to ch-1 sp at corner, (2 dc, ch 1, 2 dc) in ch-1 sp] 4 times, dc in next 2 dc, join with sl st in first dc—464 dc. Finish off.

RND 4: Join Black Plum with sl st in first dc of Rnd 3, ch 1, [sc in each dc across to ch-1 sp at corner, (sc, ch 1, sc) in ch-1 sp at corner] 4 times, sc in next 4 dc, join with sl st in first sc—472 sc.

RNDS 5 AND 6: Ch 1, [sc in each sc across to ch-1 sp at corner, (sc, ch 1, sc) in ch-1 sp at corner] 4 times, sc in each sc across, join with sl st in first sc—488 sc after Rnd 6.

RND 7: [Sl st in each sc across to next ch-1 sp, ch 1] 4 times, sl st in each sc across, join with sl st in center of first sl st—488 sl st. Fasten off and weave in all ends.

Tip
To help join squares evenly, use stitch markers to mark center of sides of body and head squares before whipstitching them to the tail square.

Layout Diagram

Clouds Removed

The irregular shading of a hand-dyed yarn such as the one featured here gives such lovely depth and texture to colorwork. Because so many of the afghans in this book are inspired by quilts, I like the idea of a yarn that is not all one solid color. The subtle color variations in this yarn are suggestive of the look of a batik fabric or the tone-on-tone patterned fabrics often seen in quilts.

Yarn
Light worsted weight (#3 Light).

Shown Here: Anzula, For Better or Worsted, Light Worsted Weight Yarn (80% superwash Merino, 10% cashmere, 10% nylon; 200 yd [182 m]/4.5 oz [127 g]): 7 skeins Seaside (light gray; A); 2 skeins each of Slate (medium gray; B), Keola (dark green; C), and Fiona (purple; D).

Hook
G/6 (4.0 mm) or hook needed to obtain gauge.

Notions
Size 16 tapestry or yarn needle; scissors; stitch markers.

Gauge
16 dc × 9 rows = 4" × 4" (10 × 10 cm).

Finished Size
Each square measures about 9¼" × 9¼" (23.5 × 23.5 cm). With a 3" (7.5 cm) border, finished blanket measures about 42" × 52½" (106.5 × 133.5 cm).

Notes
- When crocheting into the side stitches on edges, always insert the hook under 2 strands of yarn.

- Leave long tails for sewing (about 2½ yd [2.3 m]) when beginning and ending each strip.

- To create smoother seams, when whipstitching strips together, be careful to match rows and work through only 1 strand of yarn on sides of stitches.

- On the first round of the border, work 36 stitches across sides of each square. Use stitch markers to mark the center and beginning of squares to help evenly distribute stitches down the sides.

- Refer to the layout diagram on page 127 for assistance.

5-Double Crochet Shell (5-dc shell)

5 dc worked into the same st.

Tips

When working into sides of strips on Rnd 1 of the border, insert hook under 2 strands from st sides and ch 1 at end and beginning of rows. Work stitches evenly by counting 36 stitches in the side of each Star square and 16 sts in the 10 non-colorwork rows between the Stars.

Pattern

Work 13 Eight-Pointed Star squares in 5 continuous strips as follows:

STRIP 1 (MAKE 3)

ROWS 1–22: Follow instructions for Eight-Pointed Star (Square #15). Do not finish off. Turn.

ROWS 23–32: With A, ch 1, dc in each dc across, turn—36 dc in A.

ROWS 33–64: Rep Rows 1–32.

ROWS 65–86: Follow instructions for Eight-Pointed Star. Finish off, leaving long tail of A for sewing strips together.

STRIP 2 (MAKE 2)

With A, ch 38.

ROWS 1–16: Dc in third ch from hook and each dc across, turn—36 A.

ROWS 17–38: Follow instructions for Eight-Pointed Star. Do not finish off. Turn.

ROWS 39–48: With A, ch 1, dc in each dc across, turn—36 A.

ROWS 49–70: Follow instructions for Eight-Pointed Star. Do not finish off. Turn.

ROWS 71–86: Rep Row 39. Finish off, leaving long tail of A for sewing strips together.

FINISHING

Weave in all ends except long tails for sewing.

Joining Strips

Use a tapestry needle to whipstitch strips together, alternating Strip 1 and Strip 2 as shown in the layout diagram. Insert needle through just 1 strand of yarn from sides of sts when joining sides of rows.

Border

Join A in corner of last row of third Strip 1 with sl st.

RND 1: Ch 1, dc in same dc, 138 dc evenly down first side to corner, 5 dc in unused lps of first beg ch, 178 dc across rem unused lps of beg chs of all 5 strips, 5 dc-shell in corner dc, work 138 dc evenly down next side, 5 dc-shell in top of corner dc, 178 dc across last rows of all 5 strips, 4 dc in first dc used, join with sl st in first dc—652 dc.

RND 2: Ch 1, [dc in first dc and each dc across to corner, 5 dc-shell in third dc of 5-dc shell] rep around, dc in next dc, join with sl st in first dc. Finish off—664 dc.

RND 3: Join B with sc in third dc of last 5-dc shell of previous rnd, [sc in each sc across to corner, 2 sc in third dc of 5-dc shell] on first 3 sides, sc in each sc across to last corner, sc in same dc as first sc, join with sl st in first sc—668 sc.

RND 4: Sl st in next 2 sc, sc in next sc, *[hdc in next 2 sc, dc in next 2 sc, hdc in next 2 sc, sc in next 2 sc] rep across to corner, (hdc, 2 dc) in next sc, (2 dc, hdc) in next sc*, [sc in next 2 sc, rep from * to *] 3 times, sc in same sc as first sl st, join with sl st in first sc—680 sts or 82 waves plus corners.

RND 5: Ch 1, dc2tog, *[dc in next hdc, 2 dc in next 2 dc, dc in next hdc, 2 dc2tog] 18 times, 2 dc in next dc, 3 dc in next 2 dc, 2 dc in next dc, 2 dc2tog, rep from [to] 23 times, 2 dc in next dc, 3 dc in next 2 dc, 2 dc in next dc*, 2 dc2tog, rep from * to *, dc2tog, join with sl st in first dc2tog. Finish off—696 dc.

RND 6: Join C with sl st in first dc2tog, ch 1, dc in same dc2tog as join, [dc in each dc and dc2tog across to first 3 dc at next corner, dc in next dc, 2 dc in next 4 dc] rep around, dc in last 4 dc, join with sl st in first dc. Finish off—712 dc.

RND 7: Join B with sl st in third dc of Rnd 6, ch 1, *[dc in same dc as join, 2 dc in next 2 dc, dc in next dc, 2 dc2tog] 18 times, **dc in next 2 dc, 2 dc in next dc, dc in next dc, 2 dc in next 4 dc, dc in next dc, 2 dc in next dc, dc in next 2 dc**, 2 dc2tog, rep from [to] 23 times, rep from ** to **, 2 dc2tog, rep from *, join with sl st in first dc2tog—728 dc.

RND 8: Ch 1, **[hdc in next 2 sc, sc in next 2 sc, hdc in next 2 sc, dc in next 2 sc] 18 times, *dc in next dc, hdc in next 3 dc, sc in next 11 dc, hdc in next 3 dc, dc in next 2 dc*, rep from [to] 23 times, rep from * to *, rep from **, join with sl st in first hdc—728 sts.

RND 9: Sl st loosely in each st around, join with sl st through center of first sl st—728 sl st. Fasten off.

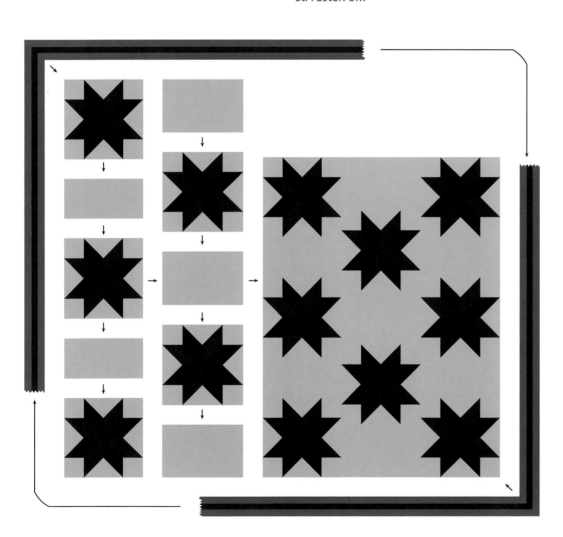

Layout Diagram

Alternative Design Idea

If you are not yet comfortable with the half-color double crochet stitches, this same layout could be made using the Double Friendship Star (Square #13). You would just need to make some adjustments to the yarn quantities and begin and end Strip 2 with 20 rows, rather than 16.

The Game's Afoot

This playful pattern of tic-tac-toe-like nine-patch quilt squares is ready for fun and games. The quilt that originally inspired this design had the same repeated colors in each of the squares over and over. But a good friend who saw me laying out the sample squares suggested that the "cards" in each Card Trick square should match the colors of the nine-patch square they were pointing to. The pattern within a pattern created by this small change really brought the design together.

Yarn
DK weight (#3 Light).

Shown Here: Crystal Palace, Cuddles DK Weight Yarn (100% micro acrylic; 131 yd [120 m]/2 oz [50 g]): 5 skeins #6124 Whipped Cream (A for all squares); 3 skeins each #6112 Navy, #6114 Byzantium (purple), #6110 Peacock Blue (teal), and #6107 Green Banana (light green).

Please Note: Yarn colors other than A are not designated here because they will vary; see the pattern for further information.

Hook
H/8 (5.0 mm) or hook needed to obtain gauge.

Notions
Size 16 tapestry or yarn needle; scissors; stitch markers.

Gauge
14 hdc × 12 rows = 4" × 4" (10 × 10 cm).

Finished Size
Each square measures about 10" × 10" (25.5 × 25.5 cm). With a 1½" (3.8 cm) border, finished blanket measures about 43" × 43" (109 × 109 cm).

Notes
- Make sure the beginning chain of each square is not too loose, or gaps will show when they are whipstitched together.

- To create smoother seams, when whipstitching squares together, work through 2 loops of top row of stitches or unused loops of beginning chains; work through only 1 strand of yarn when joining sides of stitches.

- Leave long tails for sewing (about 24–48" [61–122 cm]) when beginning and ending each square.

- When crocheting into the side stitches on edges, always insert the hook under 2 strands of yarn.

- On first round of the border, work 36 stitches across sides of each square and between squares. Use stitch markers to mark center and beginning of squares to help evenly distribute stitches down sides.

- Refer to the layout diagram on page 131 for assistance.

Pattern

Complete 8 each of Nine-Patch (Square #2) and Card Trick (Square #14) in the following colors:

Color Combo 1 (make 2 of Square #2 and 2 of Square #14)

Color B: Byzantium

Color C: Navy

Color D: Green Banana

Color E: Peacock Blue

Color Combo 2 (make 2 of Square #2 and 2 of Square #14)

Color B: Navy

Color C: Byzantium

Color D: Peacock Blue

Color E: Green Banana

Color Combo 3 (make 2 of Square #14)

Color B: Byzantium

Color C: Navy

Color D: Peacock Blue

Color E: Green Banana

Color Combo 4 (make 2 of Square #14)

Color B: Navy

Color C: Byzantium

Color D: Green Banana

Color E: Peacock Blue

Color Combo 5 (make 2 of Square #2)

Color B: Peacock Blue

Color D: Byzantium

Color Combo 6 (make 2 of Square #2)

Color B: Green Banana

Color D: Navy

JOINING SQUARES AND FINISHING

Weave in all ends on each square, except the long tails left for sewing. Steam- or wet-block each square, paying special attention to the corners of the "cards" on the Card Trick squares.

Joining Squares

Arrange the squares as shown in the layout diagram. Using the long tails at the beginning and end of each square, join the squares by whipstitching them together. For horizontal seams, insert the needle under both lps of the top row of the bottom square and the unused lps of the beg ch of the square above it. For vertical seams, insert the needle under just 1 strand of yarn on side sts of rows. Be careful to match the rows and sts in each square and always work in the same direction for consistency of sts.

Border

Join A in upper corner of last row of last strip with sl st.

RND 1: Ch 1, sc in same st, *work 142 sc evenly into sides of sts to next corner, 3 sc in top of corner st*, 142 sc across rem unused lps of beg ch to corner, 3 sc in last st at corner, rep from * to *, 142 sc in each st across tops of strips, 2 sc in first sc used, join with sl st in first dc. Do not turn—580 sc.

RND 2: Ch 1, hdc in first st, [hdc in each st across to corner, 4 hdc in second st at corner] rep around, hdc in any remaining sts, join with sl st in first hdc—592 hdc.

RND 3: Ch 1, hdc in first hdc, [hdc in each hdc across to corner, 3 hdc in third hdc at corner] rep around, hdc in rem hdcs, join with sl st in first hdc—600 hdc.

RND 4: Rep Rnd 2—612 hdc.

RND 5: Ch 1, [sc in each hdc across to corner, 3 sc in second hdc at corner] 4 times, sc in rem hdc, join with sl st in first sc—620 sc.

RND 6: [Sl st in each sc across to third sc at corner, ch 1] 4 times, sl st in rem sc across, join with sl st in center of first sl st—620 sl st. Fasten off and weave in all ends.

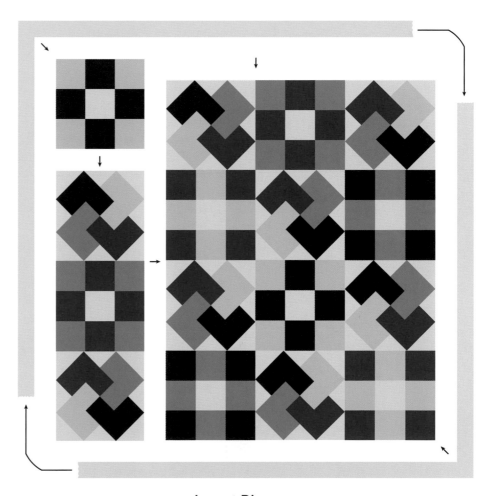

Layout Diagram

Yarn Management
AND OTHER HINTS

With the multiple strands used in colorwork, yarn management is an important part of the reversible intarsia process.

WEAVING IN ENDS

There are many ways to weave in ends, and every crocheter has his or her own tricks. Here are some things that I have found helpful for colorwork, while still keeping the stitches reversible.

- Whenever possible, carry yarn ends under several stitches of the same color as you work.

- Always leave at least a couple inches to be woven back in the opposite direction with a yarn needle, which helps to "anchor" the yarn end.

- Insert needle under the front loop of the stitch between the insertion points of two stitches and back in the other direction several inches to anchor the end (Figure 1).

- Work under the bottoms of stitches and the loops between the stitches of the row below to hide the yarn most effectively.

- Give the remaining yarn end a tug to see if it is anchored.

- Trim the ends close to your work, then stretch the fabric a little bit to pull any remaining ends inside your stitches.

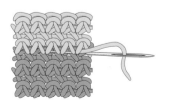

Figure 1

TROUBLESHOOTING

- If the yarn is not anchored (as described in previous bullets), try weaving in under more stitches in the opposite direction.

- If the end is too short, you can insert the needle first, then thread the needle to pull the short end through.

- In smaller sections of color, carry your ends vertically up to the next row inside the stitches.

- When working more complex design details (such as those in Square #28: Robot) you can do a little "embroidery" with the ends as you weave them in, filling any gaps and making smoother lines on your image.

TIPS AND TRICKS

- Be careful not to split the yarn with your needle as you weave in ends, as it may be noticeable in the finished product.

- Remember to check both sides of your work to be sure that you cannot see the needle before pulling the yarn through.

- Make sure you are not going through a stitch made by the same yarn end, which might undo part of your stitching. This is most important when moving vertically through your design.

- Remember to work ends *only* under stitches of the same color.

YARN PREPARATION

Many yarns come in center-pull skeins, which may work just fine for intarsia, especially if you are making many squares in the same colors for an afghan. Just remember to wrap the outer end of the yarn tightly around or place the yarn into a yarn holder (see photo on page 9). Either option will help to hold a yarn ball together so that you have to pull to get the yarn out, keeping the balls closer to your work so they don't get as tangled.

If you have more than one section and only one skein or very large skeins of yarn, it will be necessary to create smaller bobbins or balls. There are small plastic bobbins many knitters use when working in intarsia, but I prefer yarn-only "bobbins" (see Butterfly Bobbins below).

Loose Lengths

For very short lengths of only 1–2 yards (91.5–183 cm), just leave the yarn loose. It's actually far easier to separate shorter lengths from the other colors when there is no ball or bobbin attached. You simply pull the yarn from where it is attached to your work and pull the whole thing up and out from the other colors before placing it at the back of your work following a color change.

Butterfly Bobbins

With slightly longer lengths of about 3–5 yards (274.5–457.5 cm), try a Butterfly Bobbin:

1. Pinch one end of yarn between your thumb and middle of your index finger, wrapping the rest of the yarn around all four fingers until you have about 5" (12.5 cm) left **(Figure 2)**.

2. Pull wrapped yarn off fingers, pinching in the middle to hold ends in place, and wrap the last few inches of yarn around the center **(Figure 3)**.

3. Use a crochet hook to pull the tail under the yarn that is wrapped around the middle **(Figure 4)**.

4. Use the beginning end of the yarn to pull from the middle when joining a new bobbin **(Figure 5)**.

Center-Pull Balls

For larger sections of color, you can form center-pull balls:

1. Hold the yarn end between your thumb and the middle of your index finger.

2. Begin wrapping the yarn around your index finger, changing the angle of the wrap every few times around **(Figure 6)**.

3. Once the ball is big enough to stay in a ball, pull it off your finger and continue wrapping the yarn evenly around the ball while turning it slowly between your fingers to avoid too many wraps in the same direction. Be careful not to lose the beginning end inside the ball **(Figure 7)**.

4. Wrap the last few rounds tightly around the center of the ball and use a crochet hook to pull the end underneath the outer wraps. Pull the outer wraps tighter as the ball gets smaller to keep the yarn from coming out too quickly **(Figure 8)**.

Calculating Yardage

If you are not sure which type of bobbin you should make for a certain section of color, there are a few ways to estimate the yardage you will need for your bobbins:

- As you are working up your gauge swatch, use a stitch marker or knot to mark 2 yards (1.8 m) of yarn.

- Count the number of stitches per 2 yards (1.8 m) of half double or double crochet, depending on what you will be using for the pattern (x = # sts per 2 yd [1.8m]).

- Refer to the stitch diagram to count how many stitches you will be making in a given color, before you finish the color, or join that color section to a larger section of the same color.

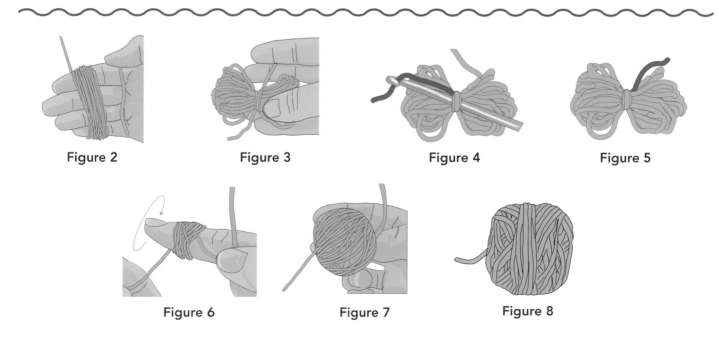

Figure 2

Figure 3

Figure 4

Figure 5

Figure 6

Figure 7

Figure 8

- Count increases and decreases as 2 stitches each (y = # of sts).

- Calculate how many yards you will need, such that y divided by x, multiplied by 2 equals the total number of yards for that section: $(y \div x)2 =$ total yards.

- Always allow at least ½–1 yard (45.5–91.5 cm) of extra yarn so you don't run out.

Note: When you are making multiples of the same square in the same colors, it is not necessary to calculate yardage and precut the yarn for each section of each square. You can simply make larger center-pull balls or bobbins for those sections of color you know you will be repeating over and over. But you do run the risk of running out in the middle of your block of color, making for more ends to weave in at the end. So try both ways to see what works best for you.

JUGGLING YARN BALLS

When one learns to juggle, one starts off with only two balls, then advances to three balls, and adds more as the skills are mastered. The squares in this book begin the same way, gradually increasing from just two colors up to as many as seven separate balls of yarn. The nine squares in the Learn Reversible Intarsia Sampler give you the opportunity to ease into working with so many different colors. Keeping so many balls or bobbins from getting completely tangled may seem rather daunting, but here are a few ways to help you keep them under control:

Containerize Them
In addition to using small bags to hold each ball of yarn, it is helpful to have a wide, shallow bag or basket with a large opening to keep all of your active yarn balls organized in your lap or on a table in front of you. This also helps to keep the balls closer to your work. The longer the lengths of yarn between your balls and your work, the more likely they are to get tangled.

Move from Front to Back
Separate each color of yarn from the rest after every color change by bringing the entire ball from the front of your work, over the top, and leaving it at the back. This will leave it ready to pick up again on the front when you turn your work for the next row. Bringing balls front to back also keeps them in the order you will be using them. To avoid all the strands twisting together when you turn your work, you can simply rotate the entire basket or bag so the opposite side is facing you, before beginning the next row.

WHEN TO CARRY YARN
When working intarsia crochet, most of the time you don't carry the unused color of yarn under the stitches as you are working. This avoids the problem of the wrong color of yarn peeking through the stitches, resulting in purer sections of color. However, in certain situations, you can carry the unused yarns to avoid needing to start a new bobbin. Just as you will hide the vertical strands of yarn inside the stitches by "flipping" the yarn up after a color change, you can sometimes hide horizontal strands by carrying them, without the carried yarns marring your blocks of color.

Carry Under or Over Stitches
You can carry any unused yarns that are the same color as the stitches directly under or above the carried yarn, without disrupting the solid blocks of color created with intarsia. Otherwise, you will need to join a new ball of yarn for each section of color.

Same Colors
When there is only a single stitch of a new color before changing back to the old color, you can carry the old color under that single stitch to cut down on yarn ends because the single stitch is worked all the way around the carried yarn. However, you will need to bring the old color forward, over the top of the carried yarn, before yarning over in the new color **(Figure 9)**. This completes the back of your stitch so that it looks like a completed stitch on both sides.

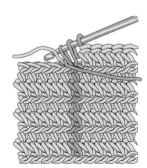

Figure 9

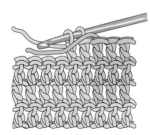

Figure 10

Bridging Over

When you change back to the first color you were using after a few stitches in a new color and that first color will be worked over the tops of those stitches on the next row:

1. Before yarning over, lay the first color yarn over the top of the stitches in the second color and wrap around to the front and under your hook **(Figure 10)**.

2. Yarn over with the first color as usual for the color change **(Figure 11)**.

3. Be sure to keep the "bridge" quite loose, so you can hide it by carrying under the stitches of the same color just before and after the bridge on the following row **(Figure 12)**.

Switchback

If either of the following are true, follow the numbered steps below: 1. You need just a couple of stitches of the first color after a few stitches of a second color, but will not need that first color on top of the stitches for the next row. 2. You are working two or more half-color double crochets, but will need the bottom color ready to pick up on the next row back at the last full double crochet in that color.

1. Create a loop of the first color, bringing yarn end up between second color and hook **(Figure 13)**.

2. Crochet over the loop with the second color for the number of stitches indicated in the pattern **(Figure 14)**.

3. Pull the loop out a bit to make sure one side of the loop is still loose. You can pull the loop larger as needed to make more stitches in the second color.

4. With the non-loose side of the loop, yarn over **(Figure 15)** and work the stitches you need in the first color, carrying the bottom strand of the loop under the stitches **(Figure 16)**.

5. Change to the next color as usual **(Figure 17)**.

6. Pull the loose end back at the beginning of the loop and tighten it to hide the loop completely under the stitches **(Figure 18)**.

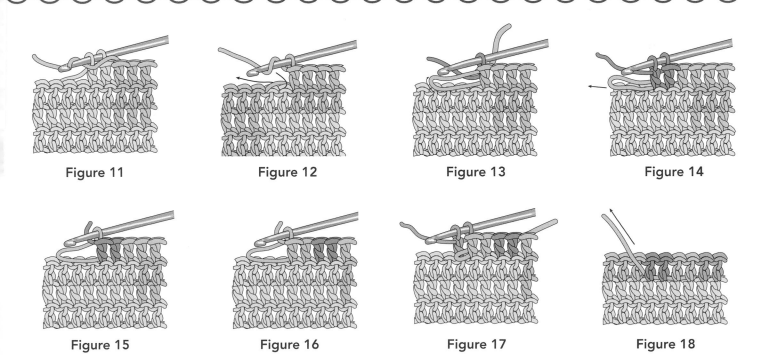

Figure 11   Figure 12   Figure 13   Figure 14

Figure 15   Figure 16   Figure 17   Figure 18

Joining a New Color

In this book, you will often be joining new colors as you work. The following information will help you get smoother stitches when joining a new color.

First Color Change in a New Color

When starting any crochet project, one typically begins with a slipknot to hold the yarn on the hook. But when it comes to adding a color or a new ball of yarn in the middle of your work, you never want those extra knots between your stitches. Simply drop the old color, form a loop with the end of the new color, and bring it over your hook as the instructions indicate (at right). Remember to leave a 4–5" (10–12.5 cm) tail to weave in later.

Multicolor Beginning Chain

For some squares, you will simply complete the beginning chain in one color. However, when the first row of the square is worked in blocks of more than one color, the instructions will tell you to "join" each new color, followed by the number of chains to be worked in that color.

"Join" a New Color in a Chain:

1. Work indicated number of chs, drop previous color and loop new color over hook, leaving a 4–5" (10–12.5 cm) tail **(Figure 19)**.

2. Ch 1 in new color **(Figure 20)**.

3. Wrap end of new color around end of previous color once, like the first half of a square knot **(Figure 21)**.

4. Pull both short ends tight (this st doesn't count as a ch). Leave ends to weave in later **(Figure 22)**.

5. Continue working indicated number of sts in new color **(Figure 23)**.

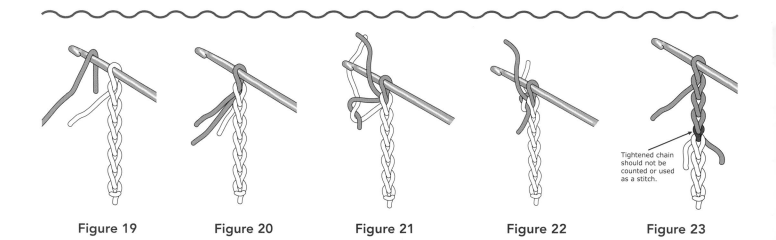

Tightened chain should not be counted or used as a stitch.

Figure 19   Figure 20   Figure 21   Figure 22   Figure 23

Troubleshooting for Reversible Stitches

Here are a few quick fixes for some common trouble spots you may come across.

LOOSE LINES

Is there a loose line of the wrong color interrupting the vertical or diagonal lines between your color changes? This is caused by the tension with which you hold the yarn. Pay special attention to keeping the first yarnover (yo) after the color change pulled tight. If you don't hold the yarn snuggly against the hook as you work the rest of the stitch, you will get these loose lines.

STRANDING

Are there short vertical or diagonal strands of yarn when you change colors? Do your color changes not look as smooth as the examples? Read about Vertical and Diagonal Stranding below for help.

Vertical Stranding

If you have upright vertical strands of yarn showing up between your color changes, this could be one of two mistakes:

- You may have forgotten to "flip" the yarn after your color change (see Forgotten Flip at right) **(Figure 24)**.

- You may be flipping yarn the wrong direction after color changes, bringing the yarn from the back of your work to the front, rather than the other way around **(Figure 25)**.

Either of these mistakes results in yarn coming around the outside of your stitches rather than being hidden inside the center of the stitch. Both are easily fixed by working the Yarn Flip (on page 19).

Diagonal Stranding

If you have diagonal strands of yarn showing up between color changes, you may be forgetting to carry the yarn under the stitch right before your color change. This is especially common when working increases and decreases. If you need more practice with when to carry yarn before a color change, review the learning squares (#5–7 for half double crochet and #9–11 for double crochet) **(Figure 26)**.

Forgotten Flip

If you get to a color change and find that the new color is at the bottom of the stitch on the previous row rather than the top, you probably forgot to flip your yarn after a color change **(Figure 27)**. If you don't want to pull out an entire row (or two), try this:

- Insert your hook through the center top of the stitch where you should have flipped and pull up a loop.

- Work a chain at the top of the row.

- Use the resulting loop after the chain as the first yarnover with the new color.

- This will not look quite as smooth as the Yarn Flip (see page 19) but allows you to avoid stranding or pulling out stitches.

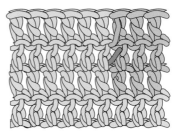
Figure 24

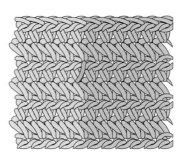
Figure 25

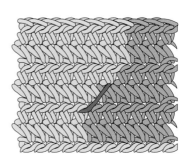
Figure 26

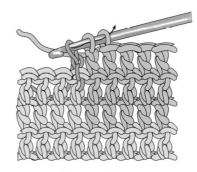
Figure 27

Glossary

Abbreviations

beg	begin/beginning
blo	through back loop(s) only
ch	chain
ch-sp	chain space
cm	centimeter(s)
dc	double crochet
dec	decrease/decreases/decreasing
flo	through front loop(s) only
fpdc	front post double crochet
g	gram(s)
hdc	half double crochet
inc	increase/increases/increasing
lp(s)	loop(s)
prev	previous
rem	remain/remaining
rep	repeat(s)
rnd	round
RS	right side
sc	single crochet
sk	skip
sl st	slip stitch
sp(s)	space(es)
st(s)	stitch(es)
tog	together
WS	wrong side
yd	yard(s)
yo	yarn over/yarnover
*	repeat instructions following asterisk as directed
**	repeat all instructions between asterisks as directed
()	alternate instructions and/or measurements
[]	work bracketed instructions specified number of times

Special Stitches Abbreviations

change to	reversible color change/double crochet reversible color change
late change to	late color change
hdc-sc-tog	hdc-sc decrease
hdc-sc-hdc-tog	hdc-sc-hdc decrease
½-color dc	half-color double crochet
rev½-color dc	reverse half-color double crochet

Blocking

For most of the afghans in this book, you can choose whether to block the individual squares or strips before joining or to join all of the squares and then block the entire afghan. One exception is The Game's Afoot afghan (page 128), because the frequent increases and decreases in the Card Trick square (#14; page 51) result in irregular edges. These irregular edges are somewhat balanced by the single crochet edging around each square in Jen and Ivo's Wedding Quilt (page 98). Without that edging, the Card Trick squares will require a little more blocking in order to achieve straight edges.

BLOCKING TOOLS

- **Straight Pins**

- **Foam Blocking Mats (or another surface for pinning into):** Many yarn stores sell blocking mats, but I have pinned into a foam mattress, an ironing board, foam puzzle pieces, and even carpet padding.

- **Clear Plastic Quilting Rulers:** These rulers are helpful for straightening edges, as well as for measuring even borders all the way around finished afghans.

- **A Hand Steamer:** An inexpensive tool you may want to have on hand if you plan to do a lot of blocking.

STEAM BLOCKING

Steam can be applied with a hand steamer or with an iron, although the steamer is more effective as it will produce more consistent moisture.

1. Fill your steamer with water and turn it on. Most steamers usually take a few minutes to turn the water into vapor.

2. Place your finished piece on the surface you plan to block on, with the wrong side up.

3. Carefully run the steam over every inch of your piece, paying special attention to the edges (which usually need the most straightening). Do not touch the steamer directly to the fabric; instead, allow a little space for the steam to come out.

4. Gently stretch out your work to smooth the stitches and edges.

5. Flip your work over to the right side and repeat the process of steaming the entire piece.

6. Pin all four corners.

7. Place one pin in the center of each side, checking that the width is the same as it was at the corners.

8. Continue pinning out from the center pins to the corners along each side, making any adjustments as necessary to create smooth, evenly spaced edges.

9. Run steam over the surface once more, focusing on the edges again.

10. Allow to dry thoroughly before removing pins.

WET BLOCKING

Wet blocking does not require any special tools but may be more difficult to manage with a large completed afghan. If you are working with wool, you may want to include a leave-in wool wash in the water.

1. Submerge your finished piece in a bath of cool water until it is damp all over.

2. Gently squeeze out excess water, but avoid twisting your work out of shape.

3. Roll the piece in a towel and press down on the roll to remove additional moisture.

4. Unroll and lay your finished work out flat.

5. Repeat Steps 6–8 of Steam Blocking for pinning.

6. Allow to dry thoroughly before removing pins.

Pinning Corners

Individual Squares: Begin by pinning at each of the four corners, measuring with a ruler to make sure the sides are even and the corners are squared up.

Full Afghans: Begin pinning one of the four corners, using a ruler to create a right angle for several pins in each direction. Repeat at all four corners, measuring each side to make sure they come out the same.

Crochet Stitches and Seams

CROCHET CHAIN (CH)

Make a slipknot and place it on crochet hook. *Yarn over hook and draw through loop on hook. Repeat from * for the desired number of stitches.

SLIP STITCH (SL ST)

*Insert hook into stitch, yarn over hook and draw loop through stitch and loop on hook. Repeat from *.

SINGLE CROCHET (SC)

Insert hook into a stitch, yarn over hook and draw up a loop **(Figure 1)**, yarn over hook and draw it through both loops on hook **(Figure 2)**.

Figure 1

Figure 2

Reverse Single Crochet (rev sc)

Working from left to right, insert hook into next stitch **(Figure 1)**, yarn over hook, draw loop of yarn to front of work, yarn over hook **(Figure 2)** and draw through both loops on hook **(Figure 3)**.

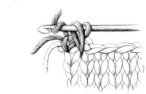

Figure 1

Figure 2

Figure 3

HALF DOUBLE CROCHET (HDC)

*Yarn over hook, insert hook into next stitch, yarn over hook and draw up a loop (3 loops on hook), yarn over hook **(Figure 1)** and draw it through all loops on hook **(Figure 2)**. Repeat from *.

Figure 1

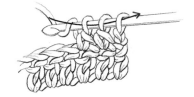

Figure 2

DOUBLE CROCHET (DC)

*Yarn over hook, insert hook into next stitch, yarn over hook and draw up a loop (3 loops on hook; **Figure 1**), yarn over hook and draw it through 2 loops **(Figure 2)**, yarn over hook and draw it through remaining 2 loops on hook **(Figure 3)**. Repeat from *.

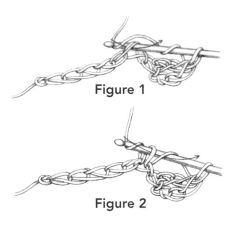

Figure 1

Figure 2

Figure 3

Double Crochet 2 Together (dc2tog)

Yarn over hook, insert hook in next stitch, yarn over hook and draw up a loop, yarn over hook and draw through 2 loops] twice (3 loops on hook). Yarn over hook, pull through all remaining loops on hook—1 decrease made.

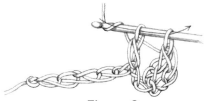

Double Crochet 3 Together (dc3tog)

[Yarn over hook, insert hook in next stitch, yarn over hook and draw up a loop, yarn over hook and draw through 2 loops] 3 times (4 loops on hook). Yarn over hook, pull through all remaining loops on hook—2 decreases made.

SLIP-STITCH SEAM

Make slipknot and place on hook. *Insert hook through edge stitches of both pieces of fabric **(Figure 1)**, wrap yarn around hook to make loop, pull loop back through fabric and through loop on hook **(Figure 2)**. Repeat from * to end of seam.

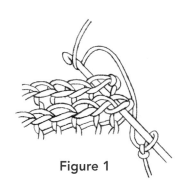

Figure 1

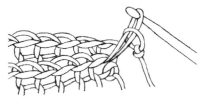

Figure 2

WOVEN STITCH

Match stitches on the 2 pieces to join. Insert the needle, from bottom to top, into the next stitch on the top piece; pull yarn through. Insert needle, from bottom to top, into the corresponding stitch on the bottom piece; pull yarn tight. Repeat across, pulling yarn tight after every few stitches.

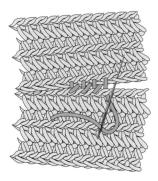

WHIPSTITCH SEAM

With right sides of work facing and working through edge stitches, bring threaded needle out from back to front, along edge of piece.

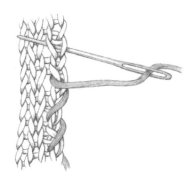

Resources

YARN

Anzula Luxury Fibers
740 H St.
Fresno, CA 93721
anzula.com
For Better or For Worsted

Berroco
PO Box 367
14 Elmdale Rd.
Uxbridge, MA 01569
(401) 769-1212
berroco.com
Comfort Worsted

Brown Sheep Company Inc.
100662 County Rd. 16
Mitchell, NE 69357
(800) 826-9136
brownsheep.com
Cotton Fleece

Cascade Yarns
PO Box 58168
Tukwila, WA 98138
(800) 548-1048
cascadeyarns.com
Pacific Chunky

Crystal Palace Yarns
Straw Into Gold Inc.
160 23rd St.
Richmond, CA 94804
straw.com
Cuddles DK

Lion Brand Yarn Co.
135 Kero Rd.
Carlstadt, NJ 07072
(800) 795-5466
lionbrand.com
Vanna's Choice

Plymouth Yarn Company Inc.
500 Lafayette St.
Bristol, PA 19007
(215) 788-0459
plymouthyarn.com
Encore Worsted

Red Heart
Coats & Clark Consumer Services
PO Box 12229
Greenville, SC 29612
(800) 648-1479
redheart.com
With Love

Sweet Georgia
110-408 East Kent Ave. S
Vancouver, BC
Canada V5X 2X7
(604) 569-6811
sweetgeorgiayarns.com
Superwash Chunky

NOTIONS

Buffy Ann Designs
762 Alaska Dr.
Santa Rosa, CA 95405
(707) 508-5028
buffyanndesigns.com
Yarn Cozy

Offhand Designs
2220 Livingston St., Ste. 204
Oakland, CA 94606
(510) 842-9411
offhanddesigns.com
Scottie handbag (for keeping yarn bobbins organized while working)

Top Shelf Totes
793 Foothill Blvd. #49
San Luis Obispo, CA 93405
(805) 776-3239
yarnpop.com
Yarn Pop Zipper Bag

CROCHET COMMUNITIES

Crochet Guild of America (CGOA)
crochet.org

Crochet Me
crochetme.com

Ravelry
ravelry.com

Crochet Liberation Front
hookey.org

Crochetville
crochetville.org